150
AMERICAN FOLK SONGS
TO SING, READ
AND PLAY

Selected and edited by

PETER ERDEI

and the Staff of the

Kodály Musical Training Institute

Collected Principally by

KATALIN KOMLOS

Library of Congress Number: 74-76415
ISBN Number: 0-913932-04-3

TXB-50

TABLE OF CONTENTS

INTRODUCTION

"Folk song grows in small steps, with every slight change tested for audience reaction, thereby achieving a permanence in men's affection matched only by the greatest art."

Preface, Folk Song USA.   (1947)
Alan Lomax

"To write a folk song is as much beyond the bounds of possibility as to write a proverb. Just as the proverbs condense the people's wisdom and observation of centuries, so in the traditional songs, the emotions of centuries live their eternal lives in a form polished to perfection."

Program Notes to the Peacock Variations.   (1950)
Zoltan Kodály

"They say it is possible to hammer a golden coin until it is large enough to cover a horseman.

In which shape is the coin worth more? Its weight remains the same, so does its value. Except it is easier to pocket the coin.

Hence, a short folk song can be just as valuable as a long-hammered piece of art music."

Lecture, Folk Music and Art Music.   (1941)
Zoltan Kodály

Considering the number of genuinely valuable folk song collections that have seen light during the last 50-60 years in the U.S., the following collection may seem quite limited. However, it must be seen as an attempt to satisfy a crying need of music educators in our schools for artistically valuable material which is appropriate and simple for vocal performance.

How often one can hear small children struggling with melodies of too big a range, too difficult intervals and rhythm. And as a result, the beauty of the song is lost, and only the memory of confusion and the feeling of strain remains with the children. Most songs in this collection are simple enough in every way for small children, and have already been successfully used.

"Folk song is the school of good taste", said Zoltan Kodály. He emphasized that education of the young must begin with his own musical mother tongue. "The musical mother tongue of a nation is the set of expressions and forms which separates the music of that nation from that of most other nations."

Preface. Collection of Songs for Schools.   (1943)
Zoltan Kodály

Through the efforts of Zoltan Kodály and Béla Bartók, the "rediscovery" of the folk-traditions of Hungary at the beginning of this century resulted in a clear picture of the Hungarian musical mother tongue. Not so easily clarified is the answer to the question, what is the musical mother tongue of the United States? What is U.S. Folk Song?

According to Alan Lomax, American folk song is a museum of musical antiques from many lands, — the mixing and blending of various folk strains to produce new forms. Examples of the strongest of these traditions may be found in this collection.

Thousands of songs were studied in choosing those deemed useful in educating the new generation in music. All songs taken from books, recording and tapes have been analyzed according to their scale, range, form, metre and rhythmic difficulty as well as their type and origin. All available variants were compared.

Finally, from among the many variants (versions) those with the most beautiful and singable melodic line and the clearest form were chosen for the early grades.

Since variants of the same song can be found in different regions of the country and this is a sign of authentic folk song, we have occasionally included two variants of some songs, if they were equally good.

This book is seen only as a beginning. There is no Spanish-American material included, very little Afro-American, no Indian. These territories will have to be researched deeply and intensively in the preparation of additional volumes.

One might ask why this collection has been done now, when the comparative work has hardly begun. Even though we have only a preliminary knowledge of the character and different streams of American folk music, it is possible to select good songs for teachers to use, but first and foremost for children to sing. This is our task.

I would like to express my deep gratitude to Miss Kati Komlos, research assistant of the Kodály Musical Training Institute, for her great contribution of collecting, analyzing and organizing folk songs, and her selflessness in helping me to copy and prepare this collection. I am also very grateful to Miss Denise Bacon, Director of the Kodály Musical Training Institute, and to Mrs. Eleanor G. Locke. Without their help and excellent suggestions this volume couldn't have been realized.

In all, every single person at the Kodály Musical Training Institute gave his or her share in preparing this collection. I thank them all.

It is hoped that these songs will be used widely and freely by all who share with Kodály and all the music teachers he inspired, a high sense of the joy of singing and the great responsibility of educating children.

Peter Erdei

April, 1972

EDITORIAL CONSIDERATIONS

In certain cases, time signatures or rhythmic notation have been changed in order to better express the natural feeling for the flow and phrasing of the song.

In every case where a song's rhythmic notation has been changed (for instance from 2/4 to 4/4, from 4/4 to ¢, from quarter and eighth notes to eighths and sixteenths, etc.) an asterisk appears above the time signature of the song.

In two cases where melodic changes are indicated, an asterisk appears above the note in question and an explanation appears at the bottom of the page.

We have not come lightly to the decision to change notation, wishing to preserve the authenticity of each song and to produce a collection representing the highest possible standard of scholarship. In no cases has any *real* change been made in either the sound or the text of a song, but only in the way it is written down. Undoubtedly, the original collectors of these songs notated them in the easiest way without thought to their eventual use in a classroom. We have also felt it wise to notate songs with similar characteristics in a similar manner for consistency's sake so that teachers wanting to use them in a certain pedagogical order will not be confused.

We would like to draw your attention to the special alignment technique used, in which every phrase begins a new line regardless of the problem of splitting measures or beats. This is not an accident but is designed to make clear the structure of the songs.

Many decisions concerning the collection had to be made after Peter Erdei's return to Hungary in June 1972. Because of copyright clearance and other problems unknown to Mr. Erdei at the time the collection was originally completed, it was necessary to substitute over a dozen new songs.

We regret that among those we felt it necessary to withdraw were some of the best and most useful songs in the collection. They came mainly from *Cecil Sharp's English Folk Songs from the Southern Appalachians*, Vols. I and II, Oxford University Press, London 1966. We urge the reader to seek out especially the following songs from this collection for himself: *Cocky Robin, Phoebe in her Petticoat, Early Sunday Morning.*

In the weekly meetings held to analyze the material which is the basis of our published curriculum, the Institute staff came up with several excellent suggestions, not only as to substitutions for the songs we had to delete from this collection, but also in the matter of building future curriculum. It was clear that the accumulated experience and weekly sharing of seven staff members currently testing material in both urban and suburban settings was an invaluable base from which we could build. In addition there is the insurmountable difficulty of communicating half way across the world in order to make decisions or changes.

While in no way diminishing the original work of Mr. Erdei and the selfless dedication of both Mr. Erdei and Miss Komlos, we would like to acknowledge the recent invaluable contribution of the KMTI teaching staff, to which we have made reference on the title page.

THE NOTATION OF THE SONGS

All songs in this collection have been transposed to end on G. This makes it easier to compare their melodic elements, and to find similarities and difficulties. This is not an indication of where to pitch them. For example No. 139, Sweet William, is notated too high for singing. A suggested starting note has been written above each song to solve this problem. For example, in the case of No. 139: comfortable starting pitch = D.

Only the sharps or flats actually used in a song appear in the key signature. This practice is suitable for Nos. 5 through 8, since the melodies consist of three tones only. Further, it recognizes the fact that much folk music is modal rather than diatonic. To determine the key or mode of a song, knowledge of a key signature and final note is not enough. It must be studied all the way to the end!

No instrumental accompaniments have been suggested to the songs. It is one of the fundamental principles of the Kodály concept that the singing voice should not be covered by a comforting curtain of instrumental sound. Accompaniment of this sort does not educate for independence, or develop pitch accuracy.

"The beginners' first steps in the endless realm of notes should be supported not by any instrument of tempered tuning and dissimilar tone color, but by another singing voice . . ."

Foreword to: Let Us Sing Correctly!
Zoltan Kodály

"The Anglo-American folksong is perhaps more widely current without than with accompaniment. Occasional accompaniment by banjo, fiddle, or dulcimer may have been traditional for a century or so. The guitar, now probably the most used, is a comparatively recent favorite."

Musical Foreword to Folk Song USA.
Charles Seeger

THE ORGANIZATION OF THE SONGS

After having chosen the songs the most difficult question was how to organize them, what criteria to use for grouping them.

They could have been arranged according to geographical areas, types, ethnic background, etc. There are a number of excellent anthologies in each of these areas; besides, the number of songs presented here is too limited to use any one of the above mentioned categories. The logical answer would have been to organize them according to a pedagogical sequence, showing an order of difficulty. But, in that case only one possibility could have been explained. For the time being, when every city – even practically every school – has a different music program, and the ratio between the frequency of music instruction and the age of the children is widely varied, a graded collection might be more confusing than useful.

The songs in this collection are grouped according to their melodic characteristics.

1. They have been divided into two large groups.
   a) songs in pentatonic scale.
   b) songs in diatonic scale.

2. The next step was to group the songs according to range. (range: the interval between the lowest and highest point of a melody). The smaller intervals precede the larger ones. For example a major 3rd (M3) would come earlier than the perfect 5th (5).

3. Next a distinction is made between melodies of identical range. The order has been made according to the number of different pitches found in a melody. The songs having fewer pitches would come first. For example, pentatonic songs with a range of a major 6th (M6) have been organized in the following manner:

l s m d (EDBG)	4 different pitches
m r d s, (BAGD)	4 different pitches
m d l, s, (BGED)	4 different pitches
l s m r d (EDBAG)	5 different pitches
m r d l, s, (BAGED)	5 different pitches

4. Within one group of songs with identical range and identical number of pitches a further distinction is made according to rhythmic difficulty. This means that songs that have only ♩ notes and ♪ notes will come earlier in the order than the ones having ♩. ♪ rhythm or ♫♫ For example, in this collection, those songs in the pentatonic scale, with the range of a 5th, having 4 different pitches (s m r d) are arranged in the following order:

   No. 12. Let Us Chase the Squirrel . . . . . has only ♩ ♫ ♩

   No. 13. Bye, Bye Baby . . . . has ♩ ♫ ♩

   No. 14. Grandma Grunts . . . . has ♩ ♫ ♩

   No. 15. Who's That Tapping at the Window . . has ♩ ♫ ♩ ♪

   No. 16. How Many Miles to Babylon . . . . has ♩ ♫ ♩ ♩ ♩.♪ ♫

   No. 18. That's a Mighty Pretty Motion . . . . . has ♩ ♫ ♩ ♪ ♩.♪ ♪♪.

Problems of pagination have occasionally required that the song be placed out of order.

The following table of the songs shows the solfa syllables, range, metre, and whether or not there is a described game included with the song.

INDEX OF SYLLABLES, RANGES, METRES AND GAMES

In the solfa syllable column the circled letter indicates the final note of the melody.

Title	Syllables	Range	Metre	Game
1. Hot Cross Buns	m r (d)	M3	4/4	
2. The Boatman	m r (d)	M3	4/4	
3. Hop Old Squirrel	m r (d)	M3	2/4	
4. The Closet Key	m r (d)	M3	2/4	X
5. Rain Rain	l s (m)	4	2/4	
6. Little Sally Water	l s (m)	4	2/4	X
7. Bye Baby Bunting	l s (m)	4	2/4	
8. A Tisket A Tasket (2)	l s (m)	4	2/4	X
9. Hunt The Slipper	d l, (s,)	4	2/4	
10. Hickety	d l, (s,)	4	6/8	X
11. Tisket A Tasket	d l, (s,)	4	2/4	X
12. Let Us Chase The Squirrel	s m r (d)	5	2/4	X
13. Bye, Bye Baby	s m r (d)	5	2/4	
14. Grandma Grunts	s m r (d)	5	2/4	
15. Who's That Tapping At The Window	s m r (d)	5	2/4	
16. How Many Miles To Babylon	s m r (d)	5	4/4	X
17. Bought Me A Cat	s m r (d)	5	2/4	
18. That's A Mighty Pretty Motion	s m r (d)	5	4/4	X
19. Rosie, Darling Rosie	m r (d) l,	5	4/4	X
20. Old Mister Rabbit	m r (d) l,	5	2/4	
21. Poor Little Kitty Puss	m r (d) l,	5	2/4	
22. Down In The Meadow	d' (l) s m	M6	4/4	
23. Peas In The Pot	d' (l) s m	M6	2/4	
24. Ring Around The Rosy (1)	l s m (d)	M6	2/4	X
25. Draw A Bucket Of Water	m r d (s,)	M6	2/4	X
26. Charlie Over The Ocean	m r (d) s,	M6	4/4	X
27. Hush Little Baby	m r (d) s,	M6	2/4	
28. Shanghai Chicken	m r (d) s,	M6	2/4	
29. The Swallow	m r (d) s,	M6	3/4-2/4	X
30. Down Came A Lady	m (d) l,,s,	M6	4/4	X
31. Kitty, Kitty Casket	m d l, (s,)	M6	2/4	
32. Bluebird	l s m r (d)	M6	4/4	X
33. Bow, Wow, Wow	l s m r (d)	M6	4/4	X
34. The Mocking Bird	l s m r (d)		4/4	
35. Rocky Mountain	l s m r (d)	M6	2/4	
36. Page's Train	l s m r (d)	M6	¢	
37. Do, Do Pity My Case	l s m r (d)	M6	2/4	
38. Ida Red	l s m r (d)	M6	2/4	
39. Mama Buy Me A Chiney Doll	l s m r (d)	M6	2/4	
40. Sally Go Round De Sun	l s m r (d)	M6	2/4	
41. There Was A Man	m r (d) l, s,	M6	2/4	
42. Ridin' Of A Goat, Leadin' Of A Sheep	m r (d) l, s,	M6	2/2	
43. Cotton Eye Joe	m r (d) l, s,	M6	¢	
44. Dog And Cat	m r (d) l, s,	M6	2/4	
45. The Jolly Miller	m r (d) l, s,	M6	¢	X
46. Old MacDonald Had A Farm	m r (d) l, s,	M6	2/4	
47. Chase The Squirrel	m r (d) l, s,	M6	2/4	

Title	Syllables	Range	Metre	Game
48. C-Line Woman	m r d (l,) s,	M6	2/4	
49. Most Done Ling'ring Here	m r d (l,) s,	M6	2/4	
50. Old Chisolm Trail	m r d l, (s,)	M6	4/4	
51. Chickalileelo	m r d (l,) s,	M6	2/4	
52. Dear Companion	m r d (l,) s,	M6	3/2	
53. Jim Along Josie	s m r (d) l,	m7	2/4	
54. Stooping On The Window	s m r d (l,)	m7	2/4	X
55. The Old Sow	s m r (d) s,	8	2/4	
56. Cock Robin	l m r d (l,)	8	2/2	
57. Little Sally Walker	s m d l, (s,)	8	¢	
58. Oh Fly Around My Pretty Little Miss	m (d) l, s, m,	8	2/4	
59. King Kong Kitchie	s m r (d) l, s,	8	¢	
60. Shoes Of John	s m r (d) l, s,	8	4/4	
61. Band Of Angels	s m r (d) l, s,	8	2/4	
62. All Night, All Day	s m r d l, s,	8	2/4	
63. Great Big Dog	s m r d l, s,	8	4/4	
64. Show Me The Way	s m r d l, (s,)	8	4/4	
65. My Horses Ain't Hungry	m r (d) l, s, m,	8	3/4	
66. Pourquoi	d' l s m r (d)	8	4/4	
67. I Lost The Farmer's Dairy Key	d' l s m r (d)	8	2/4	X
68. The Old Woman And The Pig	d' l s m r (d)	8	¢	
69. Old Turkey Buzzard	d' l s m r (d)	8	2/4	
70. Riding In The Buggy	d' l s m r (d)	8	2/4	
71. 'Liza Jane	d' l s m r (d)	8	2/4	
72. My Good Old Man	l s m r d (l,)	8	2/4	
73. Christ Was Born	l s m r d (l,)	8	3/4	
74. Old Lady Sittin' In The Dining Room	l s m (d) l, s,	M9	¢	X
75. The Farmer In The Dell	l s m r (d) s,	M9	6/8	X
76. Mister Rabbit	l s m r (d) s,	M9	2/4	
77. Dance Josey	l s m r (d) l, s,	M9	2/4	
78. Hold My Mule	l s m r (d) l, s,	M9	2/4	
79. The Riddle Song	l s m r d l, (s,)	M9	4/4	
80. Turn The Glasses Over	l s m r (d) l, s,	M9	4/4	X
81. Sailing On The Ocean	l s m r (d) l, s,	M9	4/4	X
82. Mary Had A Baby	l s m r (d) l, s,	M9	¢	
83. Walk Along, John	l s m r (d) l, s,	M9	4/4	
84. Mister Frog Went A-Courting	l s m r (d) l, s,	M9	¢	
85. The Cherry Tree Carol	l s m r (d) l, s,	M9	3/4	
86. The Derby Ram	l s m r (d) l, s,	M9	6/8	
87. Swing Low, Sweet Chariot	l s m r (d) l, s,	M9	4/4	
88. Wayfaring Stranger	l s m r d (l,) s,	M9	3/2	
89. The Colorado Trail	d' l s m r (d) l,	m10	4/4	
90. Train Is A-Coming	d' l s m r (d) l, s,	11	¢	
91. Johnny Come Down To Hilo	d' l s m r (d) l, s,	11	¢	
92. Cape Cod Girls	d' l s m r (d) l, s,	11	¢	
93. Sourwood Mountain	d' l s m r (d) l, s,	11	¢	
94. Buy A Penny Ginger	r (d) t, s,	5	4/4	X
95. Aunt Rhody	s f m r (d)	5	¢	
96. The Deaf Woman's Courtship	s f m r (d)	5	2/4	
97. Oats And Beans	s f m r (d)	5	6/8	X
98. Let's Go To The Woods	s f m r (d)	5	6/8	
99. When The Train Comes Along	m r d t, (l,)	5	¢	
100. Old Bald Eagle	m r d t, s,	M6	2/4	X

INDEX OF SONGS

m r d

Hot Cross Buns

Comfortable Starting Pitch: A

♩ = 112

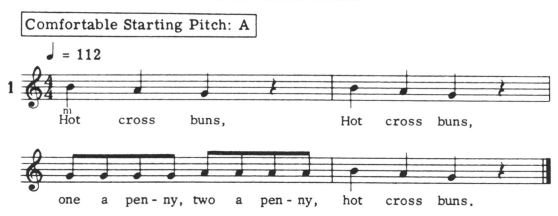

Hot cross buns, Hot cross buns,

one a pen-ny, two a pen-ny, hot cross buns.

The Boatman

CSP: F

Afro-American

♩ = 160

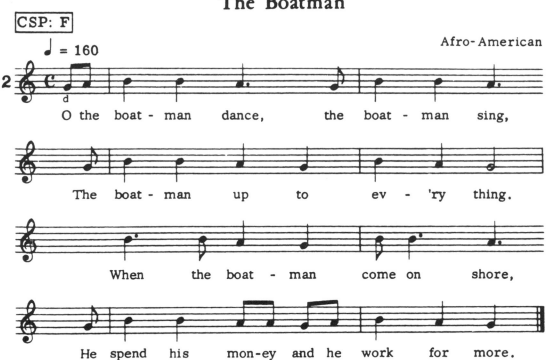

O the boat-man dance, the boat-man sing,

The boat-man up to ev-'ry thing.

When the boat-man come on shore,

He spend his mon-ey and he work for more.

2. Did you ever see where the boatman live?
His house in the hollow with a roof like a sieve!
Boatman say he got one wish.
If it gets much wetter he's going to be a fish.

3. The oyster boat should keep to shore
The fishing smack should venture more
The sailing ship go before the wind,
The steamboat leave a trail behind.

Hop Old Squirrel

Afro-American

Hop old squirrel, eidledum, eidledum, Hop old squirrel, eidledum aum,

Hop old squirrel, eidledum, eidledum, Hop old squirrel, eidledum dee!

The Closet Key

Game Song

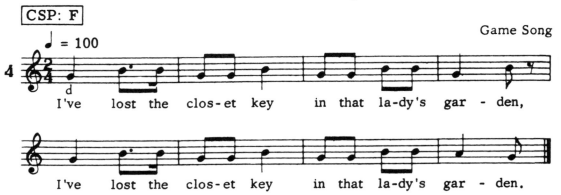

I've lost the clos-et key in that la-dy's gar - den,

I've lost the clos-et key in that la-dy's gar - den.

2. Help me find the closet key in that lady's garden,
   Help me find the closet key in that lady's garden.

3. I've found the closet key in that lady's garden,
   I've found the closet key in that lady's garden.

Game

Very small children use this song for hiding and finding play. Other children play it as indicated in the folklore collection in which it was found. Children form a ring, hands behind their backs. One child walks around and places the key in someone's hand. The walker leads the singing of stanzas 1 and 2 (with all children joining in.) The child to whom the key was given then leads the singing of stanza 3 (with all the children joining in.) He then proceeds to walk around the ring himself, singing stanza 1, and the whole process is repeated.

l s m

Rain Rain

CSP: A

♩ = 88

Rain, rain, go a-way, Come a-gain some oth-er day.

Little Sally Water

Game Song

CSP: A

♩ = 104

Lit-tle Sal-ly Wa-ter sit-ting in a sau-cer,

Rise Sal-ly, rise Sal-ly, wipe a-way your tears, Sal-ly,

Turn to the east, Sal-ly, Turn to the west, Sal-ly,

Turn to the one, that you love the best Sal-ly.

Game

Children join hands in a circle, with one child in the center as "Sally", covering his or her eyes with two hands. The circle moves around as they sing the song. The child in the center imitates the song all the way through, pointing to another child in the circle at the end of the song, still covering the eyes with one hand, so that the choice is accidental. The chosen child becomes "Sally", goes to the center and the game starts again.

4

Bye, Baby Bunting

CSP: A

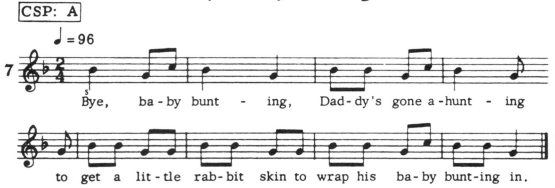

Bye, ba-by bunt - ing, Dad-dy's gone a -hunt - ing

to get a lit-tle rab-bit skin to wrap his ba-by bunt-ing in.

A Tisket A Tasket

CSP: E

Game Song

A tis - ket a tas - ket, a green and yel-low bas - ket

I wrote a let-ter to my love and on the way I dropped it,

I dropped it, I dropped it, and on the way I dropped it.

Game

Children form a circle. One child circles outside the ring, carrying a handkerchief. At the very end of the song he drops it behind a child in the ring and starts to run around the ring. The child who has the handkerchief at his heels must pick it up and run after the first child. If he catches the first child before he completes the circle to the empty place, the first child must go around again. If he does not catch the first child, he must go around, and the game begins again.

d l, s

Hunt The Slipper

CSP: A

Jamaican

Cob-bler, cob-bler, make my shoe, let it done by half past two.

Half past two is at the door, let it done by half past four.

Hickety

CSP: A

Alabama - Game Song

Hick - e - ty, hick - e - ty hor - ny cup

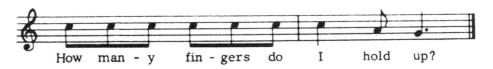

How man - y fin - gers do I hold up?

The child answers: "Two"

Spoken: "Two you said and three there were."

Sung: "Hickety, hickety horny cup,
How many fingers do I hold up."

Game

Hold the child across your knees in a spanking position. As you sing, hold up a number of fingers. The child guesses how many you are holding up.

For instance, you held up three fingers and child answers: "Two". You reply: "Two you said and three there were". Then sing it again and repeat until child guesses correctly.

6

Tisket, A Tasket

Afro-American - Game Song

CSP: A

♩ = 140

Tis - ket a tas - ket

I made a lit-tle bas - ket,

I wrote a let - ter to my love

And on the way I dropped it, ___ dropped it. ___

*Originally in 4/4

Game

This is a form of drop-the-handkerchief. The players were not at all sure of the words. Some said, "I wrote a little basket," others said – "I made a little basket". The latter would make better sense, but the majority sang it as given here.

s m r d

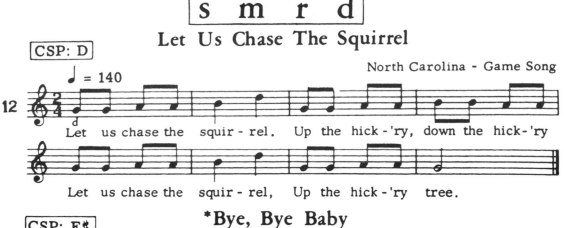

Let Us Chase The Squirrel

North Carolina - Game Song

CSP: D

♩ = 140

Let us chase the squir - rel. Up the hick - 'ry, down the hick-'ry

Let us chase the squir - rel, Up the hick - 'ry tree.

*Bye, Bye Baby

Appalachian

CSP: F♯

♩ = 80

Bye, bye ba - by, ba - by bye,

My lit - tle ba - by, ba - by bye.

Grandma Grunts

Who's That Tapping At The Window?

How Many Miles To Babylon?

Game Song

Game

The players form into two rows facing each other, each row singing its own line. For the "beck" those in row 1 bend back, and for the "bow" they bow forward. At the demand "Open the Gates" those in row 2 form an arch.

Row 1 now becomes Row 2 - the players forming the arch become row 1 and the game restarts.

Bought Me A Cat

CSP: D

♩ = 160

17

1. Bought me a cat, the cat pleas'd me; Fed my cat under yonder tree.
2. Bought me a hen, the hen pleas'd me; Fed my hen under yonder tree.
3. Bought me a duck, the duck pleas'd me; Fed my duck under yonder tree.
4. Bought me a goose, the goose pleas'd me; Fed my goose under yonder tree.
5. Bought me a dog, the dog pleas'd me; Fed my dog under yonder tree.
6. Bought me a sheep, the sheep pleas'd me; Fed my sheep under yonder tree.
7. Bought me a cow, the cow pleas'd me; Fed my cow under yonder tree.
8. Bought me a horse, the horse pleas'd me; Fed my horse under yonder tree.
9. Bought me a baby, the baby pleas'd me; Fed my baby under yonder tree.
10. Bought me a woman, the woman pleas'd me; Fed my woman under yonder tree.

1a. Cat went fid-dle-i-fee.

2a. Hen went chip-sy chop-sy,
3a. Duck went sli-shy slo-shy,
4a. Goose went qua,
5a. Dog went bow,
6a. Sheep went baa,
7a. Cow went moo,
8a. Horse went neigh,
9a. Baby went mom-my, mom-my,
10a. Woman went hon-ey, hon-ey,

After each verse repeat, backwards, all of the preceding numbers in this column, ending up with 1a.

That's A Mighty Pretty Motion

CSP: F#

♩ = 168

Afro-American - Game Song

18

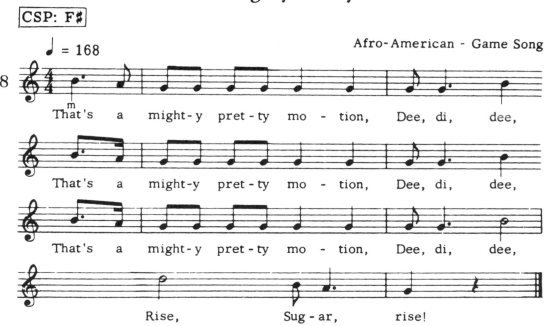

That's a might-y pret-ty mo - tion, Dee, di, dee,

That's a might-y pret-ty mo - tion, Dee, di, dee,

That's a might-y pret-ty mo - tion, Dee, di, dee,

Rise, Sug - ar, rise!

2. That's a mighty poor motion, Dee, di, dee,
That's a mighty poor motion, Dee, di, dee,
That's a mighty poor motion, Dee, di, dee,
Rise, Sugar, rise.

(Second Version)

1. That's a very pretty motion, Tra, la, lut,
That's a very pretty motion, Tra, la, lut,
That's a very pretty motion, Tra, la, lut,
Rise, Sugar, rise.

2. That's a very poor motion, Tra, la, lut,
That's a very poor motion, Tra, la, lut,
That's a very poor motion, Tra, la, lut,
Rise, Sugar, rise.

Game

The children stand in a large circle with hands unjoined. One child is in the center at the beginning of the song and makes any motion he or she wishes to the words ---"That's a mighty pretty motion, Dee, di, dee." These motions are usually some type of dance step in the rhythm of the music. The children clap vociferously on the first and third beats throughout.

At the words, "Rise, Sugar, rise," center child selects another who enters the ring while she takes the selected child's place in the circle.

On the second verse, the child in the center makes any grotesque or humorous motions he or she wishes. Sometimes this is sung and acted out at the end of "Rise, Sugar, rise" and in other localities it is a play-song by itself.

m r d l,

Rosie, Darling Rosie

CSP: D

♩ = 126

Afro American - Game Song

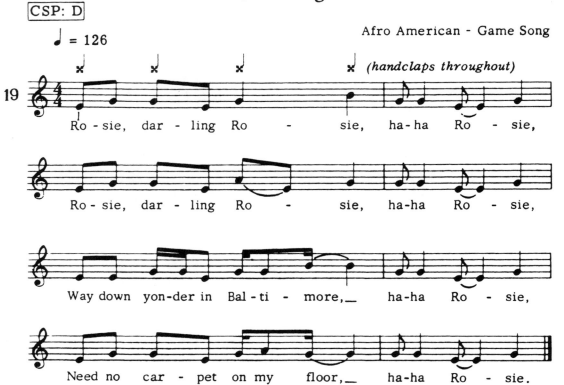

Ro - sie, dar - ling Ro - sie, ha - ha Ro - sie,

Ro - sie, dar - ling Ro - sie, ha - ha Ro - sie,

Way down yon-der in Bal - ti - more,__ ha - ha Ro - sie,

Need no car - pet on my floor,__ ha - ha Ro - sie.

2. Grab your partner and follow me, ha-ha Rosie

   Let's go down by Galilee, ha-ha Rosie

   Rosie darling hurry, ha-ha Rosie

   If you don't mind you gonna get left, ha-ha Rosie.

3. You steal my partner, you won't steal her no more, ha-ha Rosie

   Better stay from round my door, ha-ha Rosie

   Stop right still and study yourself, ha-ha Rosie

   See that fool where she got left, ha-ha Rosie.

Game

The children form two circles, one within the other. As a partner is chosen, the pair skips around between the two circles — the erstwhile leader then takes his place in the vacated spot, and the one he has chosen becomes the new leader.

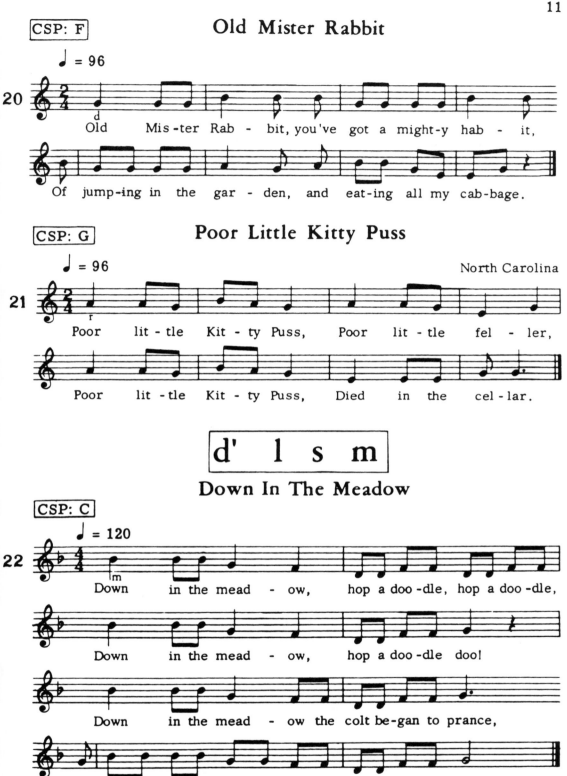

2. Down in the barnyard, hop a doodle, hop a doodle!
Down in the barnyard, hop a doodle doo!
Down in the barnyard the goose began to sing
The hen began to cackle as the rooster flapped a wing.

Peas In The Pot, Hoe Cake A-Bakin'

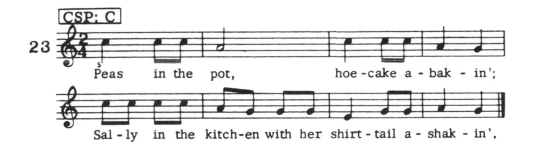

CSP: C

23

Peas in the pot, hoe-cake a-bak-in';

Sal-ly in the kitch-en with her shirt-tail a-shak-in'.

l s m d

Ring Around The Rosy

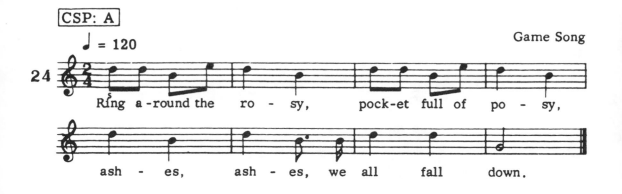

CSP: A

♩ = 120

Game Song

24

Ring a-round the ro-sy, pock-et full of po-sy,

ash-es, ash-es, we all fall down.

Game

Children join hands in a circle and walk around singing the song.

At the word "down" they all squat down on their heels, then immediately get up, and the game starts again.

m r d s,

Draw A Bucket Of Water

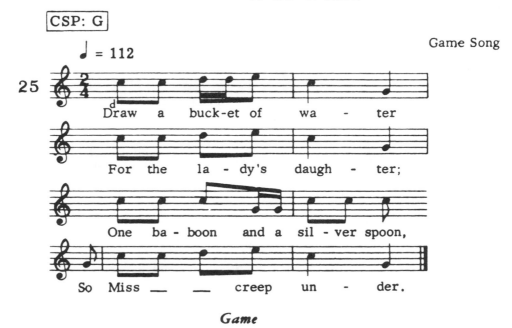

CSP: G

Game Song

♩ = 112

25

Draw a buck-et of wa - ter

For the la - dy's daugh - ter;

One ba - boon and a sil - ver spoon,

So Miss — — creep un - der.

Game

Formation: *Four children form a simple circle, boy (1), girl (2), boy (3), girl (4), or 4 boys or 4 girls. The children standing opposite to each other join both hands straight across, forming a square of 4 arms and hands.*

Action: *On the 1st beat of each measure No. 1 and No. 2 pull or No. 3 and No. 4 push; on the 2nd beat of each measure the action is reversed. At the end of the verse, No. 1 and No. 3 raise the joined right hand of No. 1 and left hand of No. 3 over the head of No. 2. The verse is sung 4 times and arms are raised over each child in turn, so as to form a tight circle with arms around each child. Now the four children in this tight circle jump up and down as they circle to the left and chant 3 times:*

"Jump, jump, Sugar, jump, you'll all jump down".

It is expected that the children will fall down before they reach the end of the chant.

Charlie Over The Ocean

CSP: G

♩ = 138

Afro-American -
Game Song

Leader, then Ring:

26

Char - lie o - ver the o - cean,

Char - lie o - ver the sea,

Char - lie caught a black bird,

Might been me.

2. *Leader* - Charlie over the ocean,
   Ring   - Charlie over the ocean,
   Leader - Charlie over the sea,
   Ring   - Charlie over the sea,
   Leader - Charlie caught a black fish,
   Ring   - Charlie caught a black fish,
   Leader - Can't catch me.
   Ring   - Can't catch me.

3. *Leader* - Charlie over the ocean,
   Ring   - Charlie over the ocean,
   Leader - Charlie over the sea,
   Ring   - Charlie over the sea,
   Leader - Charlie caught a blackbird,
   Ring   - Charlie caught a blackbird,
   Leader - Can't catch me.
   Ring   - Can't catch me.

Game

The children join hands in a ring and skip to their right. The leader, who is outside, skips in the opposite direction. He begins the song and the ring sings each line back to him. As the leader says "Charlie caught a blackbird" he touches one of those in the ring and begins to run around the ring. The child who was touched tries to catch him. If the leader can get around the ring to the empty place, the other child becomes the leader. If not, he remains on the outside. The song continues and all children take part as the leader.

This game is almost the same as the more familiar Drop the Handkerchief, but all the children take part, either by their singing or by the more active part of the ring. (In Drop the Handkerchief the circle does not move.)

Another way of playing this game is for the leader to be in the center of the circle, blindfolded. On the line "Charlie caught a blackbird", the circle squats, moving about from side to side, as the leader attempts to find one of the children.

Hush Little Baby

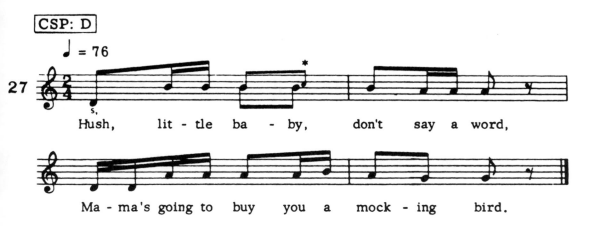

CSP: D

♩ = 76

27

Hush, lit - tle ba - by, don't say a word,

Ma - ma's going to buy you a mock - ing bird.

2. If that mocking bird won't sing
   Mama's going to buy you a diamond ring.

3. If that diamond ring turns brass,
   Mama's going to buy you a looking glass.

4. If that looking glass gets broke,
   Mama's going to buy you a billy goat.

5. If that billy goat won't pull,
   Mama's going to buy you a cart and bull.

6. If that cart and bull turn over,
   Mama's going to buy you a dog named Rover.

7. If that dog named Rover won't bark,
   Mama's going to buy you a horse and cart.

8. If that horse and cart fall down,
   You'll still be the prettiest girl in town.

*Though no source has been found with the C notation, one usually hears it with C rather than B.

Shanghai Chicken

CSP: G

♩ = 112

Minstrel Song

28

Shang - hai chick-en and he grow so tall, Hoo - day! Hoo - day!

Take that egg a month to fall, Hoo - day! Hoo - day!

The Swallow

CSP: G

♩ = 108

Afro - American - Game Song

29

Lit-tle swal-low, fly to your nest, Who goes there, fly a fly a - way now.

Lit-tle swal-low, fly to your nest, fly a fly a - way.

Game

A circle is formed with one child outside (the swallow). The children hold hands and walk around singing, while the swallow runs quickly around the outside and drops a handkerchief behind any child he or she chooses. Each child is on the watch, and as soon as the handkerchief is found at his feet, picks it up and runs after the swallow, who usually manages to get to the gap left in the circle before the pursuer catches him. If caught, he in turn becomes the swallow.

m d l, s,

Down Came A Lady

CSP: F

Game Song

♩ = 120

30

Down came a la - dy, down came two,

Down came old Dan- iel's wife and she was dressed in blue.

Game

All except one child join hands in a circle. The remaining child stands in center. All sing, circling around center child, who at "blue" points to one of the other children substituting the color of the chosen child's clothing for the word "blue". That child goes outside the circle and, when singing begins again, walks in opposite direction to original circle. This continues until all children are in outside circle.

On last verse, children in circle point to center child and shout color of his clothing.

Kitty, Kitty Casket

CSP: G

Afro-American

♩ = 116

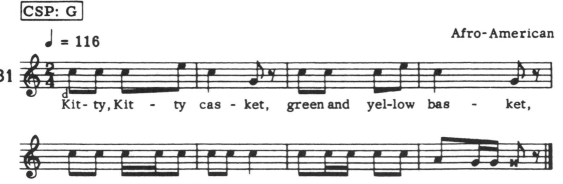

31

Kit- ty, Kit - ty cas - ket, green and yel-low bas - ket,

lost my handkerchief yesterday, s'all full of mud I tossed it a-way.

l s m r d

Bluebird

CSP: A

Game Song

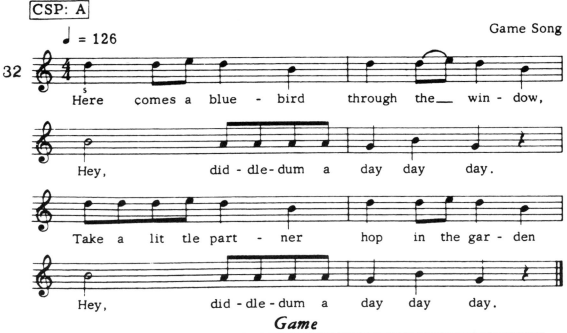

32

Here comes a blue - bird through the__ win - dow,

Hey, did - dle - dum a day day day.

Take a lit tle part - ner hop in the gar - den

Hey, did - dle - dum a day day day.

Game

The children stand, with hands joined in a ring. One child walks in and under the arches. On "take a little partner" this child takes a part- ner and with two hands joined they face each other and gallop out through the opening where the child was taken from the ring, and back again - or dance the same around inside the ring. The first child joins the ring, the partner becomes the bluebird.

Bow, Wow, Wow

CSP: E

Game Song

33

Bow, wow, wow, whose dog art thou?

Lit - tle Tom - my Tuck-er's dog bow, wow, wow.

Game

Bow, wow, wow	- *stamp 3 times (right, left, right)*
Whose	- *clap hands*
dog art thou?	- *with a jerk point right forefinger upward, raising it about nose high*
Little Tommy Tucker's dog	- *partners clasp hands and quickly circle in place.*
Bow, wow, wow	- *stamp 3 times turning away from partner and facing neighbor.*

The Mocking Bird

Rocky Mountain

2. Sunny valley, sunny valley, sunny valley low,
   When you're in that sunny valley, sing it soft and slow.
   Do, do, do, do, do remember me.
   Do, do, do, do, do remember me.

3. Stormy ocean, stormy ocean, stormy ocean wide,
   When you're on that deep blue sea, there's no place you can hide.
   Do, do, do, do, do remember me.
   Do, do, do, do, do remember me.

Page's Train

CSP: F♯

North Carolina

♩ = 112

36

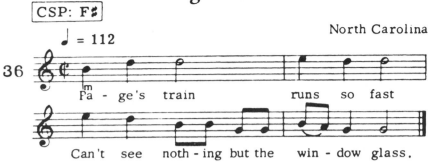

Pa - ge's train   runs   so   fast
Can't   see   noth - ing but the   win - dow glass.

Do, Do, Pity My Case.

CSP: F♯

♩ = 90

37

Do,   do,   pit - y   my   case,
In   some   la - dy's   gar   -   den.
My clothes to wash when   I   get   home,—
In   some   la - dy's   gar   -   den.

2. Do, do, pity my case
   In some lady's garden
   My clothes to iron when I get home,
   In some lady's garden.

*And so on, the performers lamenting the duty which lies
upon them (scrubbing their floors, baking their bread, etc.)*

*Originally ⁴₄

Ida Red

CSP: D

Kentucky

♩ = 104

38

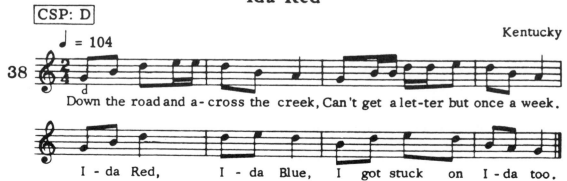

Down the road and a - cross the creek, Can't get a let-ter but once a week.
I - da Red,   I - da Blue,   I got stuck   on I - da too.

Mama, Buy Me A Chiney Doll

2. (Well) What would it take to buy it with? *(Sing 3 times)*
   Do, mammy, do.

3. You could take daddy's feather bed *(Sing 3 times)*
   Do, mammy, do.

4. Then where would our daddy sleep? *(Sing 3 times)*
   Do, mammy, do.

5. He could sleep in the puppy's bed *(Sing 3 times)*
   Do, mammy, do.

6. Then where would our puppy sleep? *(Sing 3 times)*
   Do, mammy, do.

7. Sleep in the horse's bed *(Sing 3 times)*
   Do, mammy, do.

8. Then where could our horsey sleep? *(Sing 3 times)*
   Do, mammy, do.

9. Sleep in the piggy's bed *(Sing 3 times)*
   Do, mammy, do.

10. Then where could our piggy sleep? *(Sing 3 times)*
    Do, mammy, do.

11. She could root out on our front lawn *(Sing 3 times)*
    Do, mammy, do.

12. Then where would our children play? *(Sing 3 times)*
    Do, mammy, do.

13. Swing on the garden gate *(Sing 3 times)*
    Do, mammy, do.

14. Yes and get a spanking too. *(Sing 3 times)*
    Do, mammy, do.

Sally Go 'Round The Sun

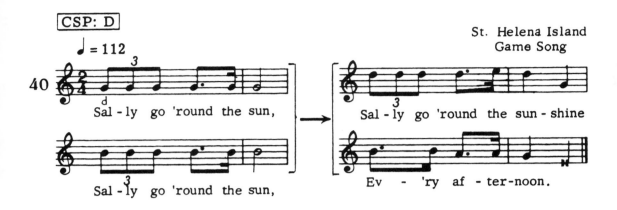

St. Helena Island
Game Song

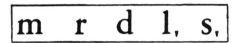

There Was A Man

2. The pudding bag it was so fine
That he jumped into a bottle of wine.

3. The bottle of wine it was so clear
That he jumped into a bottle of beer.

4. The bottle of beer it was so thick
That he jumped into a walking stick.

5. The walking stick it was so narrow
That he jumped into a wheel barrow.

6. The wheel barrow it did so crack
That he jumped onto a horse's back.

7. The horse's back it did so bend
That he jumped into a touching end.

8. The touching end it was so rotten
That he jumped into a bag of cotton.

9. The bag of cotton it set on fire
And blow him up to Jeremiah!

Ridin' Of A Goat, Leadin' Of A Sheep

North Carolina

Rid-in' of a goat and lead-in' of a sheep,

Rid-in' of a goat and lead-in' of a sheep,

Rid-in' of a goat and lead-in' of a sheep,

I won't be back 'till the mid-dle of the week.

Cotton Eye Joe

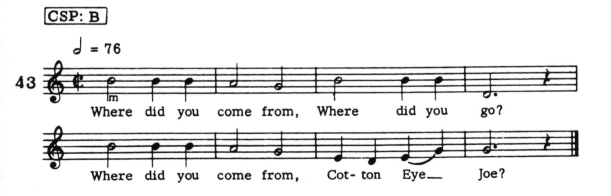

Where did you come from, Where did you go?

Where did you come from, Cot-ton Eye__ Joe?

2. Come for to see you, come for to sing,
   Come for to show you my diamond ring.

Dog And Cat

CSP: F

44 ♩ = 76

Bought me a dog, bought me a cat.

They both fight but do not mind that.

Hi - o my dar - ling.

2. Bought me a coat, bought me a hat,
   They don't fit but do not mind that.
   Hi-o my darling.

*Originally in 4/4

The Jolly Miller

CSP: D

Game Song

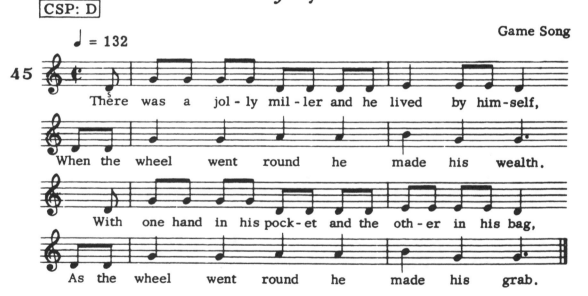

45 ♩ = 132

There was a jol - ly mil - ler and he lived by him-self,

When the wheel went round he made his wealth.

With one hand in his pock - et and the oth - er in his bag,

As the wheel went round he made his grab.

Game.

This is played by an uneven number of children. They divide into couples and, hand in hand (or arm in arm) form a ring, the odd child (the Miller) standing in the center. All sing the verse, walking around, suggesting the mill wheel. At the end of the verse every inside partner steps quickly forward and catches the outside partner of the pair in front. While this is going on, however, the Miller tries to seize one of the outside ring and get a partner for himself. This enables him to join the ring. The one child left without a partner becomes the Miller and the game recommences.

Old MacDonald Had A Farm

CSP: G

♩ = 108

2. Old MacDonald had a farm,
   E - I - E - I - O.
   And on that farm he had some ducks,
   E - I - E - I - O.
   With a quack-quack here, and a quack-quack there,
   Here a quack, there a quack, everywhere a quack-quack,
   Chick-chick here, and a chick-chick there,
   Here a chick, there a chick, everywhere a chick-chick.
   Old MacDonald had a farm,
   E - I - E - I - O.

This song can be continued with as many animals and their noises that you can think of, or until you drop from exhaustion.

Chase The Squirrel

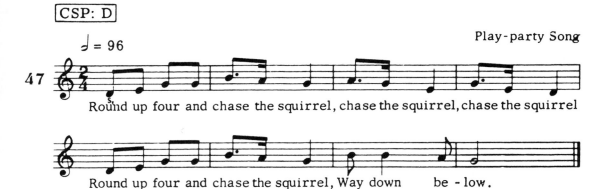

CSP: D

♩ = 96

Play-party Song

47

Round up four and chase the squirrel, chase the squirrel, chase the squirrel
Round up four and chase the squirrel, Way down   be - low.

2. Break and swing and chase the squirrel,
   Chase the squirrel, chase the squirrel,
   Break and swing and chase the squirrel,
   Way down below.

3. Round up six and chase the squirrel,
   Chase the squirrel, chase the squirrel,
   Round up six and chase the squirrel,
   Way down below.

4. Break and swing and chase the squirrel,
   Chase the squirrel, chase the squirrel,
   Break and swing and chase the squirrel,
   Way down below.

5. Round up eight and chase the squirrel,
   Chase the squirrel, chase the squirrel,
   Round up eight and chase the squirrel,
   Way down below.

C-Line Woman

CSP: B

Afro-American

♩ = 108

48

C - line wom - an, Ce - la,

She drink cof - fee, Ce - la,

She drink tea, Ce - la,

In the can - dle light, Ce - la,

2. Way down yonder, Cela,
On the log, Cela,
And the rooster crowed, Cela,
In the candlelight, Cela.

Most Done Ling'ring Here

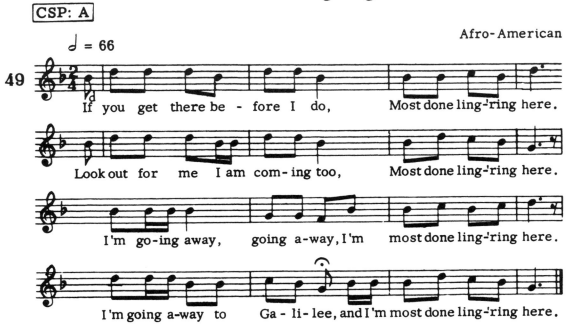

CSP: A

Afro-American

♩ = 66

49

If you get there be - fore I do, Most done ling-'ring here.

Look out for me I am com - ing too, Most done ling-'ring here.

I'm go - ing away, going a-way, I'm most done ling-'ring here.

I'm going a-way to Ga - li - lee, and I'm most done ling-'ring here.

Old Chisolm Trail

CSP: A

♩ = 138   Western

50

Come a-long boys and lis-ten to my tale,

I'll tell you of my trou-bles on the old Chi-solm Trail,

Come a ti yi yip-py yip-py yea yip-py yea,

Come a ti yi yip-py yip-py yea.

2. I started up the trail October 23rd
   I started up the trail with the two U herd.
   Come a ti yi yippy yippy ye yippy yea
   Come a ti yi yippy yippy yea.

3. I woke one morning on the Chisolm Trail
   Rope in my hand and a cow by the tail
   Come a ti yi yippy yippy ye yippy yea
   Come a ti yi yippy yippy yea.

4. Cloudy in the west, and it looks like rain
   My darned old slicker's in the wagon again.
   Come a ti yi yippy yippy yea yippy yea
   Come a ti yi yippy yippy yea.

5. I went to the boss to draw out my roll
   He figured me out nine dollars in the hold.
   Come a ti yi yippy yippy yea yippy yea
   Come a ti yi yippy yippy yea.

6. Going to sell my outfit just as quick as I can
   And I won't punch cows for any man.
   Come a ti yi yippy yippy yea yippy yea
   Come a ti yi yippy yippy yea.

7. With my knees in the saddle and my seat in the sky,
   I'll quit punching cows in the sweet by and by.
   Come a ti yi yippy yippy yea yippy yea
   Come a ti yi yippy yippy yea.

Chickalileelo

CSP: E

Southern

♩ = 100

51

La   la   la chick-a - li - lee - o,   La la la-chick-a - li-lee-o.

I'm goin' to mar-ry   who I please, La la la-chick-a - li-lee-o.

2. I'll bet you I will if you marry me,
   La, la chickalileelo.
   La, la chickalileelo,
   La, la chickalileelo.

3. Now I'm goin' to marry little Johnny Green,
   La, la chickalileelo.
   He's the prett'est boy I've ever seen,
   La, la chickalileelo.

4. But he's gone off to the war away,
   La, la chickalileelo.
   He come back some pretty fair day,
   La, la chickalileelo.

5. La, la chickalileelo
   La, la chickalileelo
   La, la chickalileelo
   La, la chickalileelo.

6. Now yonder he comes I do believe,
   La, la chickalileelo.
   I hope he'll marry me,
   La, la chickalileelo.

7. La, la chickalileelo
   La, la chickalileelo
   La, la chickalileelo
   La, la chickalileelo.

Dear Companion

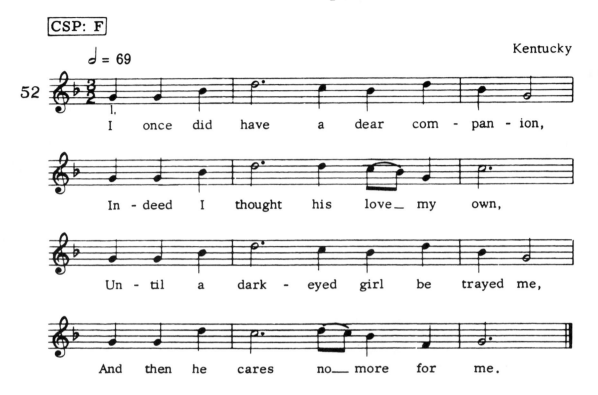

CSP: F

♩ = 69

Kentucky

52

I once did have a dear com - pan - ion,

In - deed I thought his love— my own,

Un - til a dark - eyed girl be trayed me,

And then he cares no— more for me.

2. Just go and leave me if you wish to.
   It will never trouble me,
   For in your heart you love another
   And in my grave I'd rather be.

3. Last night you were sweetly sleeping,
   Dreaming in some sweet repose,
   While I, a poor girl, broken hearted,
   Listened to the wind that blows.

4. When I see your babe a-laughing,
   It makes me think of your sweet face;
   But when I see your babe a-crying,
   It makes me think of my disgrace.

s m r d l,

Jim Along Josie

CSP: B

♩ = 84

Oklahoma

53

Hey jim a - long, — jim a - long Jo - sie,

Hey jim a - long, — jim a - long Jo.

Hey jim a - long, — jim a - long Jo - sie,

Hey jim a - long, — jim a - long Jo.

2. Walk jim along, jim along Josie,
Walk jim along, jim along Jo.
Walk jim along, jim along Josie,
Walk jim along, jim along Jo.

3. Hop jim along, jim along Josie,
Hop jim along, jim along Jo.
Hop jim along, jim along Josie,
Hop jim along, jim along Jo.

Stooping On The Window

CSP: F

Afro-American - Game Song

54

Stoop - ing on the win-dow, Wind the ball -

Stoop - ing on the win-dow, Wind the ball -

Stoop - ing on the win-dow, Wind the ball -

1. Stoop - ing on the win-dow, Wind the ball -

2. Wind the ball,

(spoken)

Let's wind the ball a - gain, a-gain, a - gain, *(Repeat as many times as necessary)*

(spoken)

Un-wind the ball, a - gain, a-gain, a - gain. *(Repeat as many times as necessary)*

Game

The children hold hands in a line, with the "ball" at one end and a pair at the other, their arms arched to form a "window". Led by the leader, the line goes under the arched hands. Usually the leader calls out the first line and is answered by the others with "Wind the ball" or "Again". Sometimes the children clap their hands instead of holding to one another. The leader takes line down to the "ball" and goes around about him, "winding the ball". When all the children are tightly pressed together in a circle, the ball is unwound by the leader, who unwinds it from the center. At the end of the game the children are in a straight line.

Sometimes, instead of one arched "window", all the children hold their arms up and the leader takes them in and out down through these windows to the foot of the line and the "ball".

s m r d s,

The Old Sow

CSP: A

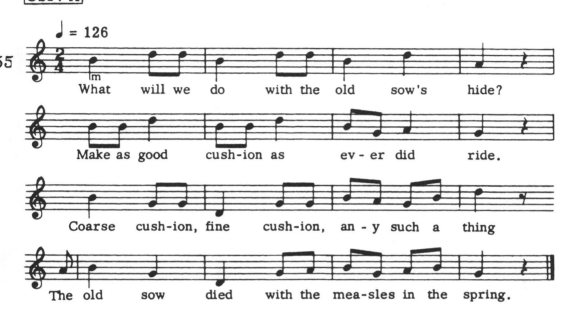

2. What will we do with the old sow's tail?
   Make as good whip as ever did sail.
   Coarse whip, fine whip, any such a thing,
   The old sow died with the measles in the spring.

3. What will we do with the old sow's meat?
   Make as good bacon as ever was eat.
   Coarse bacon, fine bacon, any such a thing,
   The old sow died with the measles in the spring.

4. What will we do with the old sow's feet?
   Make as good pickles as ever was eat.
   Coarse pickles, fine pickles, any such a thing,
   The old sow died with the measles in the spring.

5. What will we do with the old sow's head?
   Make as good oven as ever baked bread.
   Coarse oven, fine oven, any such a thing,
   The old sow died with the measles in the spring.

34

l m r d l,
Cock Robin

CSP: G

Appalachian

♩ = 76

56

Who killed Cock _ Ro - bin?

Who killed Cock _ Ro - bin?

"I," said the spar - row, "With my lit - tle bow and ar - row,

It was I, Oh, _ it was I."

s m d l, s,
Little Sally Walker

CSP: G

Afro-American - Game Song

♩ = 80

57

Lit tle Sal - ly Walk - er, sit - tin' in a sau - cer,

cry - in' for the old man to come for the dol - lar.

Rise Sal - ly, rise, put your hands on your hips, _ oh let your

back bone slip, ah,

Shake it to the east, ah, shake it to the west, ah,

Shake it to the ver - y one you love the best.

Oh, Fly Around My Pretty Little Miss

CSP: A

Western - Play-party Song

58

2. Every time I go that road
It looks so dark and dreary (hazy)
Every time I go that road
I go to see my daisy.

3. If I had no horse at all
I'd be found a-crawlin'
Up and down the rocky branch
A-huntin' for my darlin'.

King Kong Kitchie

2. Rode 'till he came to Miss Mousie's door,
   King Kong Kitchie Kitchie Kimeo
   There he knelt down on the floor,
   King Kong Kitchie Kimeo.

Shoes Of John

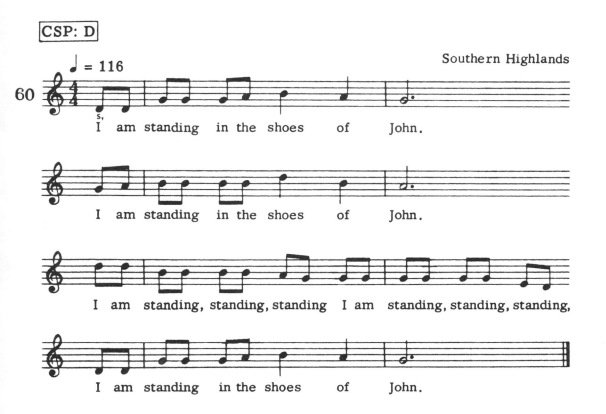

I am standing in the shoes of John.

2. If they fit me, I will put them on,
   If they fit me, I will put them on,
   If they fit me, fit me, fit me,
   If they fit me, fit me, fit me,
   If they fit me I will put them on.

3. I am going up to get my crown,
   I am going up to get my crown,
   I am going, going, going,
   I am going, going, going,
   I am going up to get my crown.

Band Of Angels

CSP: D

Carolina Spiritual

♩ = 108

61

There was one, there were two, there were three lit-tle an-gels,

There were four, there were five, there were six lit-tle an-gels,

There were seven, there were eight, there were nine lit-tle an-gels,

Ten lit - tle an-gels in that band. ___

Oh was-n't that a band Sun - day morn-ing,

Sun - day morn - ing, Sun - day morn-ing

Was-n't that a band Sun - day morn-ing

Sun - day morn - ing soon. ___

All Night, All Day

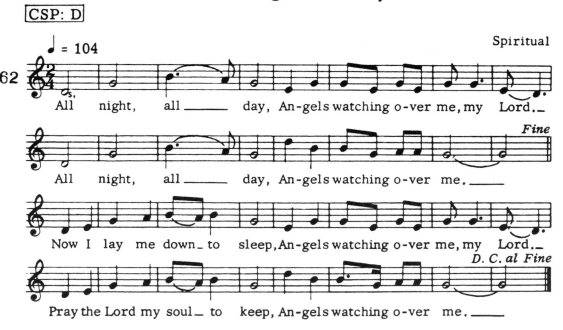

2. All night, all day
   Angels watching over me, my Lord.
   All night, all day
   Angels watching over me.
   If I die before I wake
   Angels watching over me, my Lord.
   Pray the Lord my soul to take
   Angels watching over me.

Great Big Dog

Show Me The Way

CSP: D

Afro-American

♩ = 100

64

I went down in the val - ley to pray,

Good Lord, show me the way. Talk - in' 'bout that

good old way, — Good Lord, show me the way.

Show me who shall wear the star - ry crown,

Good Lord, show me the way. Show me the way, oh

show me the way, Good Lord, show me the way.

m r d l, s, m,

My Horses Ain't Hungry

CSP: A

♩ = 132

65

My hors - es ain't hun - gry, they won't eat your hay,

So I'll get on my po - ny, I'm go - ing a - way.

2. I know you're my Polly,
   I'm not going to stay,
   So come with me, darling,
   We'll feed on our way.

3. With all our belonging,
   We'll ride till we come
   To a lonely little cabin,
   We'll call it our home.

d' l s m r d

Pourquoi

West Virginia

CSP: A

♩ = 144

66

"Oh," said the Black - bird sit-ting on a tree,

"I had a wife as well as thee,

But she flew a - way and nev - er came back,

And ev - er since then my head's been black."

2. "Oh", said the Redbird, sitting on a tree,
   "I had a wife as well as thee
   But she grew fickle and away she fled
   And ever since then my head's been red."

3. "Oh", said the Bluebird, sitting on a tree,
   "I had a wife as well as thee
   But she grew fickle and away she flew
   And ever since then my head's been blue."

4. "Oh", said the Greenbird, sitting on a tree,
"I had a wife as well as thee
But she flew away and never was seen
And ever since then my head's been green."

5. "Oh", said the Whitebird, sitting on a tree,
"I had a wife as well as thee,
But she eloped on a stormy night
And ever since then my head's been white."

6. "Oh", said the Graybird, sitting on a tree,
"I had a wife as well as thee,
But she grew fickle and flew away
And ever since then my head's been gray."

7. "Oh", said the Yellowbird, sitting on a tree,
"I had a wife as well as thee,
But she flew away with another fellow
And ever since then my head's been yellow."

8. "Oh", said the Brownbird, sitting on a tree,
"I had a wife as well as thee,
But she flew away into the town,
And ever since then my head's been brown."

I Lost The Farmer's Dairy Key

CSP: D

♩ = 104

Afro-American - Game Song

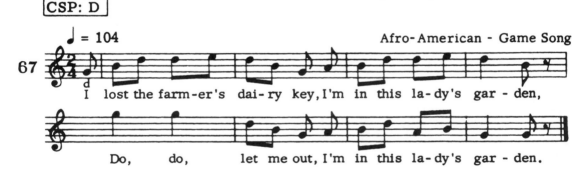

67

I lost the farm-er's dai-ry key, I'm in this la-dy's gar-den,

Do, do, let me out, I'm in this la-dy's gar-den.

2. A brass key and a silver lock,
I'm in this lady's garden,
Do, do, let me out,
I'm in this lady's garden.

3. Corn stalk fiddle and a shoe string bow,
I'm in this lady's garden,
Do, do, let me out,
I'm in this lady's garden.

Game

Children form circle with one child in center. They walk around singing until "Do, do, let me out". The one in the middle tries to break out. Second and third verses sung if necessary until he breaks out, and other child goes to center.

The Old Woman And The Pig

There was an old wom-an and she had a lit-tle pig,_ oink, oink, oink.

There was an old wom-an and she had a lit-tle pig,

He did-n't cost much 'cause he was-n't ver-y big,_ oink, oink, oink.

2. This little old woman kept the pig in a barn,
Oink, oink, oink.
This little old woman kept the pig in a barn,
The prettiest thing she had on the farm,
Oink, oink, oink.

3. But that little pig did a heap of harm,
Oink, oink, oink.
But that little pig did a heap of harm,
He made little tracks all around the barn,
Oink, oink, oink.

4. The little old woman fed the pig on clover,
Oink, oink, oink.
The little old woman fed the pig on clover,
And when he died, he died all over,
Oink, oink, oink.

Old Turkey Buzzard

North Carolina

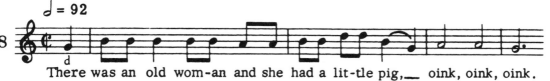

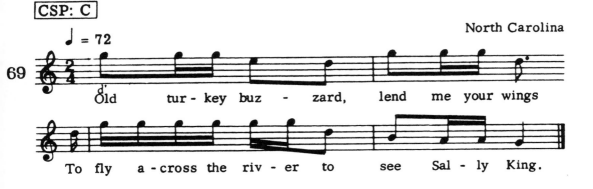

Old tur - key buz - zard, lend me your wings

To fly a - cross the riv - er to see Sal - ly King.

Riding In The Buggy

CSP: E

♩ = 102

Western - Play-party Song

70

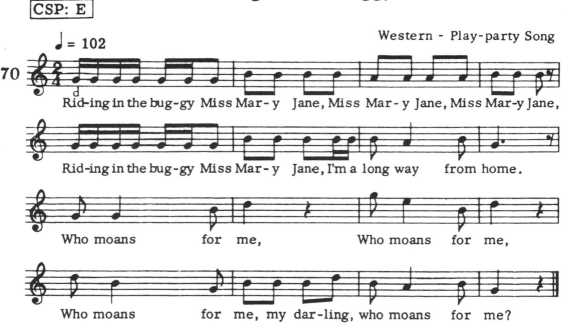

Rid-ing in the bug-gy Miss Mar-y Jane, Miss Mar-y Jane, Miss Mar-y Jane,

Rid-ing in the bug-gy Miss Mar-y Jane, I'm a long way from home.

Who moans for me, Who moans for me,

Who moans for me, my dar-ling, who moans for me?

2. Sally's got a house in Baltimore
   In Baltimore, in Baltimore.
   Sally's got a house in Baltimore
   And it's full of chicken pie.
   Who moans for me,
   Who moans for me,
   Who moans for me, my darling,
   Who moans for me?

3. I've got a girl in Baltimore
   In Baltimore, in Baltimore,
   I've got a girl in Baltimore
   And she's sixteen stories high.
   Who moans for me,
   Who moans for me,
   Who moans for me, my darling,
   Who moans for me?

4. Fare you well, my little bitty Ann,
   Little bitty Ann, little bitty Ann,
   For I'm going away.
   Who moans for me,
   Who moans for me,
   Who moans for me, my darling,
   Who moans for me?

'Liza Jane

2. I've got a house in Baltimore, Little 'Liza Jane
   Street car runs right by my door, Little 'Liza Jane.
   O, Eliza, Little 'Liza Jane.
   O, Eliza, Little 'Liza Jane.

3. I've got a house in Baltimore, Little 'Liza Jane
   Brussels carpet on the floor, Little 'Liza Jane.
   O, Eliza, Little 'Liza Jane..
   O, Eliza, Little 'Liza Jane.

4. I've got a house in Baltimore, Little 'Liza Jane
   Silver doorplate on the door, Little 'Liza Jane
   O, Eliza, Little 'Liza Jane,
   O, Eliza, Little 'Liza Jane.

l s m r d l,

My Good Old Man

CSP: D

72

♩ = 138

Where are you go - ing my good old man?

Where are you go - ing my su - gar, my lamb?

Best old man in the world._____

(Spoken: To Market)

2. What will you buy there, my good old man?
   What will you buy there, my sugar, my lamb?
   Best old man in the world.
   (Spoken) Bushel of eggs.

3. Bushel will kill you, my good old man,
   Bushel will kill you, my sugar, my lamb,
   Best old man in the world.
   (Spoken) Don't care if it does.

4. What for to die my good old man?
   What for to die my sugar, my lamb?
   Best old man in the world.
   (Spoken) So I can haunt you.

5. Why will you haunt me, my good old man?
   Why will you haunt me, my sugar, my lamb?
   Best old man in the world.
   (Spoken) So I can always be near you.

Christ Was Born

CSP: D

♩ = 88

73

Christ was born in Beth - le - hem,

In a low - ly sta - ble lay.

Born to save the souls of men,

Peace on earth this Christ-mas day.

2. Son of Mary, Lord is He,
Christ was born in Bethlehem.
Son of Mary, Lord is He,
Come to save us all from sin.

l s m d l, s,

Old Lady Sittin' In The Dining Room

CSP: G

Afro-American - Game Song

♩ = 100

74

Old La-dy sit-tin' in the din-ing room,

Sit-tin' by the fi - re,

Her foot slipped and she fell down,—

Rise up high-er and high - er.

2. Choose the one the ring go round,
   Choose the one the morning,
   Choose the one with the coal black hair,
   And kiss her and call her honey.

Game

The players join hands in a ring and skip about, while the player in the center acts out the words; squatting, falling, choosing and kissing a partner. The game is repeated, with the one chosen taking the center, while the other joins the ring.

l s m r d s,

The Farmer In The Dell

CSP: C

Game Song

♩. = 112

75

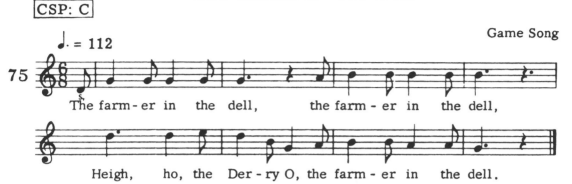

The farm-er in the dell, the farm-er in the dell,

Heigh, ho, the Der-ry O, the farm-er in the dell.

2. The farmer takes a wife,
   The farmer takes a wife,
   Heigh, ho, the Derry O,
   The farmer takes a wife.

3. The wife takes the child,
   The wife takes the child,
   Heigh, ho, the Derry O,
   The wife takes the child.

4. The child takes the nurse,
   The child takes the nurse,
   Heigh, ho, the Derry O,
   The child takes the nurse.

5. The nurse takes the dog,
   The nurse takes the dog,
   Heigh, ho, the Derry O,
   The nurse takes the dog.

6. The dog takes the cat,
   The dog takes the cat,
   Heigh, ho, the Derry O,
   The dog takes the cat.

7. The cat takes the rat,
   The cat takes the rat,
   Heigh, ho, the Derry O,
   The cat takes the rat.

8. The rat takes the cheese.
   The rat takes the cheese,
   Heigh, ho, the Derry O,
   The rat takes the cheese.

9. The cheese stands alone,
   The cheese stands alone,
   Heigh, ho, the Derry O,
   The cheese stands alone.

Game

The farmer is chosen by a counting-out rhyme. He stands in the center of the circle of players, who sing and revolve about him. He slowly turns and leisurely chooses the "wife". The player singled out leaves the circle to stand with him in the center. It is then her turn to choose the "child" and so on until the cheese is chosen. At this point the other players leave the cheese alone in the center and return to the circle. The "Cheese" then becomes the "farmer", etc.

Mister Rabbit

CSP: B

Afro-American

76

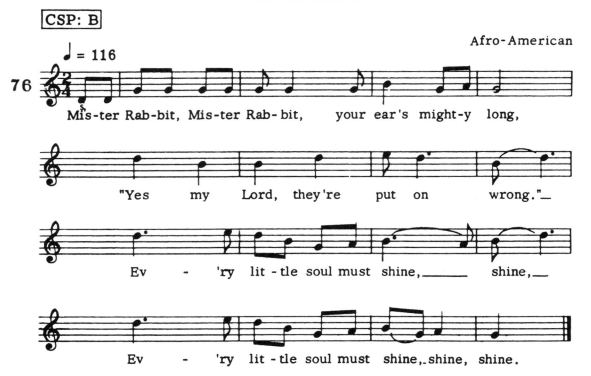

Mis-ter Rab-bit, Mis-ter Rab-bit, your ear's might-y long,

"Yes my Lord, they're put on wrong."__

Ev - 'ry lit-tle soul must shine,_____ shine,__

Ev - 'ry lit-tle soul must shine,_shine, shine.

2. Mister Rabbit, Mister Rabbit, your foot's mighty red,
   "Yes my Lord, I'm almost dead."
   Every little soul must shine, shine,
   Every little soul must shine, shine, shine.

3. Mister Rabbit, Mister Rabbit, your coat's mighty grey,
   "Yes my Lord, 'twas made that way."
   Every little soul must shine, shine,
   Every little soul must shine, shine, shine.

4. Mister Rabbit, Mister Rabbit, your tail's mighty white,
   "Yes my Lord, an' I'm gettin' out o' sight."
   Every little soul must shine, shine,
   Every little soul must shine, shine, shine.

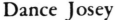

Dance Josey

CSP: F

Play-party Song

Chick-en in the fence post, can't dance Jo - sey,

Chick-en in the fence post, can't dance Jo - sey,

Chick-en in the fence post, can't dance Jo - sey,

Hel - lo Su - san Brown - y - o.

2. Choose your partner and come dance Josey, *(Sing 3 times)*
Hello Susan Browny-o.

3. Chew my gum while I dance Josey, *(Sing 3 times)*
Hello Susan Browny-o.

4. Shoestring's broke and I can't dance Josey, *(Sing 3 times)*
Hello Susan Browny-c.

5. Hold my mule while I dance Josey, *(Sing 3 times)*
Hello Susan Browny-o.

6. Crank my fad while I dance Josey, *(Sing 3 times)*
Hello Susan Browny-o.

7. Hair in the butter, can't dance Josey, *(Sing 3 times)*
Hello Susan Browny-o.

8. Briar in my heels, can't dance Josey, *(Sing 3 times)*
Hello Susan Browny-o.

9. Stumped my toe, can't dance Josey, *(Sing 3 times)*
Hello Susan Browny-o.

52

CSP: C

Hold My Mule

Afro-American

♩ = 92

78

Hold my mule while I dance Jo - sey, Hold my mule while I dance Jo - sey,

Hold my mule while I dance Jo - sey, Oh Miss Su - san Brown.

2. Wouldn't give a nickel if I couldn't dance Josey
Wouldn't give a nickel if I couldn't dance Josey
Wouldn't give a nickel if I couldn't dance Josey
Oh, Miss Susan Brown.

3. Had a glass of buttermilk and I danced Josey
Had a glass of buttermilk and I danced Josey
Had a glass of buttermilk and I danced Josey
Oh, Miss Susan Brown.

CSP: C

The Riddle Song

Southern Mountains

♩ = 88

79

I gave my love a cher - ry that has no stone,

I gave my love a chick - en that has no bone,

I gave my love a ring that has no end,

I gave my love a ba - by, there's no cry - en.

2. How can there be a cherry that has no stone?
How can there be a chicken that has no bone?
How can there be a ring that has no end?
How can there be a baby, there's no cryen?

3. A cherry when it's blooming, it has no stone,
A chicken when it's pipping, it has no bone,
A ring when it's rolling, it has no end,
A baby when it's sleeping, there's no cryen.

Turn The Glasses Over

CSP: F

Game Song

♩ = 144

80

I've been to Haar - lem, I've been to Do - ver,

I've trav-elled this wide world all o - ver,

o - ver, o - ver, three times o - ver,

Drink all the brand-y wine, and turn the glass-es o - ver.

Sail - ing east, sail - ing west,

Sail - ing o'er the o - cean,

Bet- ter watch out when the boat be - gins to rock,

Or you'll lose your girl in the o - cean.

Game

Children take partners, boys on girls' left, cross hands as in skating position and walk around, counter clockwise, in a circle while singing the first part of this song. When they reach the word "over" partners "wring the dish rag", that is, raise their crossed hands while each child turns completely around without dropping his partner's hands. This movement is repeated twice. It can be quickly mastered with a little practice.

After the double bar, hands are dropped and the boys make a circle inside the girls' circle. The boys move around in clockwise direction while the girls continue counterclockwise. At the end of the song, boys choose the girls they are nearest and the dance begins again.

Sailing On The Ocean

CSP: G

Game Song

♩ = 138

81

Sail - ing on the o - cean, the tide rolls high,

Sail - ing on the o - cean, the tide rolls high,

Sail - ing on the o - cean, the tide rolls high,

You can get a pret-ty girl, by and by.

2. Got me a pretty girl, stay all day,
   Got me a pretty girl, stay all day,
   Got me a pretty girl, stay all day,
   We don't care what the others say.

3. Eight in the boat and it won't go 'round,
   Eight in the boat and it won't go 'round,
   Eight in the boat and it won't go 'round,
   You can have the pretty girl you just found.

Game

Single circle with four boys in center.

ACTION

1. *Players in the outside circle join hands and circle clockwise while the boys in the center face toward the outer circle, join hands, and circle counterclockwise.*
2. *All players drop hands and both circles walk counterclockwise; each boy in center chooses from the outside circle the girl who is nearest him and walks beside her until end of the verse.*
3. *Each boy in the center pulls his partner into the inner circle and moves counterclockwise, while the outer circle moves clockwise. On the word "leave" the boy leaves his partner in the center and goes to the outside circle. The game is repeated with the girls in the center and the words are changed by substituting "handsome boy" for "pretty girl".*

Mary Had A Baby

CSP: F

Spiritual

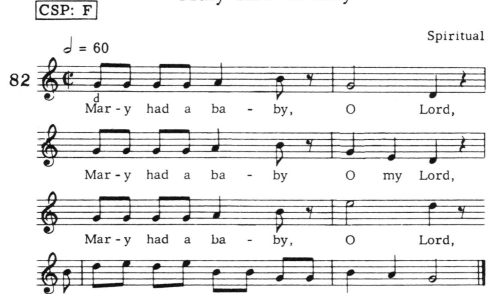

♩ = 60

82

Mar - y had a ba - by, O Lord,

Mar - y had a ba - by O my Lord,

Mar - y had a ba - by, O Lord,

The peo-ple keep a-com-ing and the train done gone.

2. What did she name him? O Lord,
   What did she name him? O my Lord;
   What did she name him? O Lord,
   The people keep a-coming and the train done gone.

3. Named him Jesus, O Lord,
   Named him Jesus, O my Lord;
   Named him Jesus, O Lord,
   The people keep a-coming and the train done gone.

4. Where was he born? O Lord,
   Where was he born? O my Lord;
   Where was he born? O Lord,
   The people keep a-coming and the train done gone.

5. Born in a stable, O Lord,
   Born in a stable, O my Lord;
   Born in a stable, O Lord,
   The people keep a-coming and the train done gone.

6. Where did they lay him? O Lord,
   Where did they lay him? O my Lord;
   Where did they lay him? O Lord,
   The people keep a-coming and the train done gone.

7. Laid him in a manger, O Lord,
   Laid him in a manger, O my Lord;
   Laid him in a manger, O Lord,
   The people keep a-coming and the train done gone.

Walk Along, John

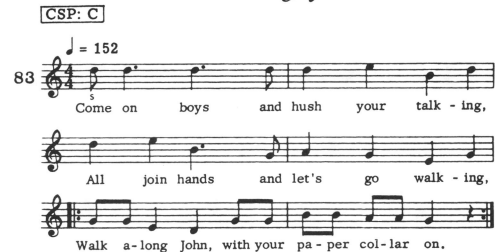

Come on boys and hush your talk-ing,
All join hands and let's go walk-ing,
Walk a-long John, with your pa-per col-lar on.

Mister Frog Went A-Courting

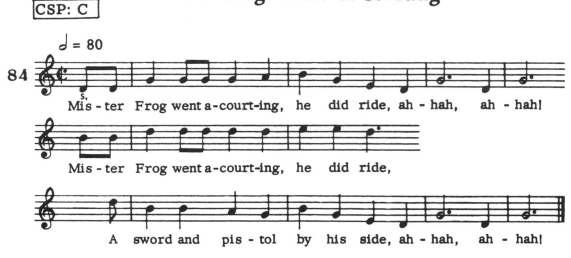

Mis-ter Frog went a-court-ing, he did ride, ah-hah, ah-hah!
Mis-ter Frog went a-court-ing, he did ride,
A sword and pis-tol by his side, ah-hah, ah-hah!

2. He rode up to Miss mousie's den,
   Ah-hah, ah-hah!
   He rode up to Miss Mousie's den,
   He said, "Miss Mouse, are you within?"
   Ah-hah, ah-hah!

3. "Oh, Mister Frog, I sit and spin,"
   Ah-hah, ah-hah!
   "Oh, Mister Frog, I sit and spin,
   Just lift the latch and please come in."
   Ah-hah, ah-hah!

4. He took Miss Mousie on his knee,
   Ah-hah, ah-hah!
   He took Miss Mousie on his knee,
   He said, "Miss Mouse, will you marry me?"
   Ah-hah, ah-hah!

5. "Without my Uncle Rat's consent,"
   Ah-hah, ah-hah!
   "Without my Uncle Rat's consent,
   I wouldn't marry the President."
   Ah-hah, ah-hah!

6. Now Uncle Rat when he came home
   Ah-hah, ah-hah!
   Now Uncle Rat when he came home
   Says, "Who's been here since I been gone?"
   Ah-hah, ah-hah!

7. "A very fine gentleman has been here
   Ah-hah, ah-hah!
   "A very fine gentleman has been here
   Who wishes me to be his dear."
   Ah-hah, ah-hah!

8. So Uncle Rat he went to town
   Ah-hah, ah-hah!
   So Uncle Rat he went to town
   To buy his niece a wedding-gown.
   Ah-hah, ah-hah!

9. Where will the wedding supper be?
   Ah-hah, ah-hah!
   Where will the wedding supper be?
   Away down yonder in a hollow tree.
   Ah-hah, ah-hah.

10. What will the wedding supper be?
    Ah-hah, ah-hah!
    What will the wedding supper be?
    Two green beans and a black-eyed pea.
    Ah-hah, ah-hah!

11. They all went a-sailing on the lake,
    Ah-hah, ah-hah!
    They all went a-sailing on the lake,
    They all were swallowed by a big black snake.
    Ah-hah, ah-hah!

12. So there's the end of one, two, three:
    Ah-hah, ah-hah!
    So there's the end of one, two, three:
    The Rat, the Frog, and Miss Mousie.
    Ah-hah, ah-hah!

13. There's bread and cheese upon the shelf;
    Ah-hah, ah-hah!
    There's bread and cheese upon the shelf;
    If you want any more, you can sing it yourself.
    Ah-hah, ah-hah!

The Cherry Tree Carol

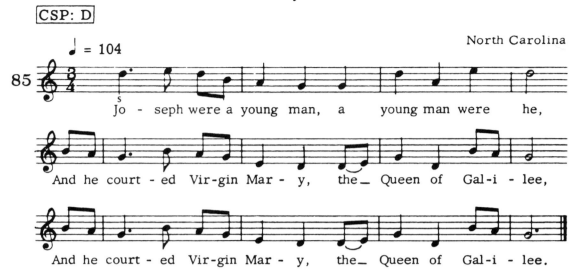

CSP: D

North Carolina

85

♩ = 104

Jo - seph were a young man, a young man were he,

And he court - ed Vir-gin Mar - y, the— Queen of Gal-i - lee,

And he court - ed Vir-gin Mar - y, the— Queen of Gal-i - lee.

2. Mary and Joseph were a-walking one day,
   "Here is apples and cherries a-plenty to behold,
   Here is apples and cherries a-plenty to behold."

3. Mary spoke to Joseph so meek and so mild,
   "Joseph, gather me some cherries for I am with child,
   Joseph, gather me some cherries for I am with child."

4. Joseph flew in anger, in anger he flew,
   Saying, "Let the father of your baby gatner cherries for you,"
   Saying, "Let the father of your baby gather cherries for you,"

5. The Lord spoke down from Heaven, these words he did say,
   "Bow you low down, you cherry tree, while Mary gathers some,"
   "Bow you low down, you cherry tree, while Mary gathers some."

6. The cherry tree bowed down, it was low on the ground
   And Mary gathered cherries while Joseph stood around,
   And Mary gathered cherries while Joseph stood around.

7. Then Joseph took Mary all on his right knee,
   "Pray tell me, little baby, when your birthday shall be,"
   "Pray tell me, little baby, when your birthday shall be."

8. "On the fifth day of January my birthday shall be
   When the stars and the elements shall tremble with fear,
   When the stars and the elements shall tremble with fear."

9. Then Joseph took Mary all on his left knee,
   Saying, "Lord, have mercy upon me, for what have I done?"
   Saying, "Lord, have mercy upon me, for what have I done?"

The Derby Ram

Ozark

Oh, as I went down to Der - by town, all on a sum-mer's day,_

It's there I saw the fin - est ram, that's ev - er fed on hay._

2. And if you don't believe me
And think I tell a lie,
Just you go down to Derby
And you'll see the same as I.

3. Oh, the wool upon this ram's back
It drug to the ground,
And I hauled it to the market
And it weighed ten thousand pounds.

4. And if you don't believe me
And think I tell a lie,
Just you go down to Derby
And you'll see the same as I.

5. Oh, the horns upon this ram's head
They reached to the moon,
For the butcher went up on February
And never got back till June.

6. And if you don't believe me
And think I tell a lie,
Just you go down to Derby
And you'll see the same as I.

7. Oh, the ears upon this ram's head
They reached to the sky,
And the eagle built his nest there
For I heard the young ones cry.

8. And if you don't believe me
And think I tell a lie,
Just you go down to Derby
And you'll see the same as I.

9. Oh,_ every tooth this ram had
Would hold a bushel of corn,
And every foot he stood on
Would cover an acre of ground.

10. And if you don't believe me
And think I tell a lie,
Just you go down to Derby
And you'll see the same as I.

Swing Low, Sweet Chariot

CSP: A

♩ = 92

87

Swing low, sweet char - i - ot, —

Com - ing for to car - ry me home.

Swing low, sweet char - i - ot, —

Fine

Com - ing for to car - ry me home.

I looked o - ver Jor - dan and what did I see, —

Com - ing for to car - ry me home.

A band of an - gels com - ing af - ter me, —

D. C. al Fine

Com - ing for to car - ry me home.

2. Swing low, sweet chariot
Coming for to carry me home
Swing low, sweet chariot
Coming for to carry me home.
If you get there before I do
Coming for to carry me home
Just tell my friends I'm coming too
Coming for to carry me home.

3. Swing low, sweet chariot
Coming for to carry me home
Swing low, sweet chariot
Coming for to carry me home
I'm sometimes up and sometimes down
Coming for to carry me home
But still my soul feels heavenly bound
Coming for to carry me home.

Wayfaring Stranger

CSP: D

White Spiritual

88

I'm just a poor way-far-ing strang-er.

A-trav'-ling through this world of woe;

But there's no sick-ness, toil nor dan-ger,

In that bright world to which I go.

I'm go-ing there to meet my fa-ther,

I'm go-ing there no more to roam,

I'm just a-go-ing o-ver Jor-dan,

I'm just a-go-ing o-ver home.

2. I know dark clouds will gather round me
I know my way is rough and steep
But beauteous fields lie just beyond me
Where souls redeemed their vigil keep.
I'm going there to meet my mother
She said she'd meet me when I come
I'm only going over Jordan
I'm only going over home.

3. I want to wear a crown of glory
When I get home to that bright land:
I want to shout Salvation's story
In concert with that Bloodwashed band
I'm going there to meet my Saviour
To sing his praise forever more
I'm only going over Jordan
I'm only going over home.

d' l s m r d l,

The Colorado Trail

Western

CSP: F#

♩ = 138

89

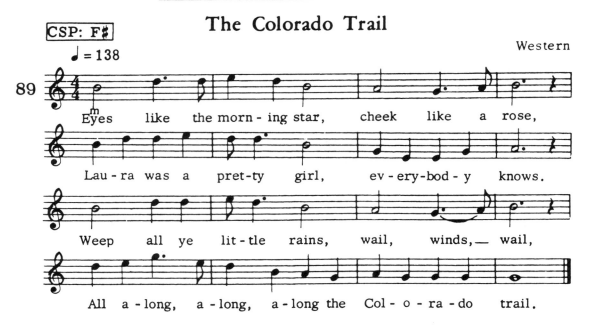

Eyes like the morn-ing star, cheek like a rose,

Lau-ra was a pret-ty girl, ev-ery-bod-y knows.

Weep all ye lit-tle rains, wail, winds,— wail,

All a-long, a-long, a-long the Col-o-ra-do trail.

d' l s m r d l, s,

Train Is A-Coming

Spiritual

CSP: E

♩ = 88

90

Train is a-com-ing, oh, yes,

Train is a-com-ing,— oh, yes,

Train is a-com-ing, train is a-com-ing,

Train is a-com-ing, oh, yes.

2. Better get your ticket, oh, yes,
   Better get your ticket, oh, yes,
   Better get your ticket,
   Better get your ticket, oh, yes.

3. Train is a-leaving, oh, yes,
   Train is a-leaving, oh, yes,
   Train is a-leaving,
   Train is a-leaving,
   Train is a-leaving, oh, yes.

Johnny Come Down To Hilo

Sailor Song

I never see the like since I been born,
Of a big black sailor with his sea boots on,
Singing, Johnny come down to Hilo,
Poor old man.
Oh, wake her, oh shake her,
Oh wake that girl with the blue dress on
Singing, Johnny come down to Hilo,
Poor old man.

Cape Cod Girls

CSP: G♯

Sea Chantey

92

Cape Cod girls they have no combs, Heave a-
way, heave a - way,
They comb their hair with cod - fish bones, We are
bound for Aus - tra - lia!
Heave a - way my bul - ly bul - ly boys, Heave a-
way, heave a - way,
Heave a - way and don't you make a noise, We are
bound for Aus - tra - lia!

2. Cape Cod boys they have no sleds
   Heave away, heave away,
   They slide down hill on codfish heads
   We are bound for Australia.
   Heave away my bully bully boys
   Heave away, heave away,
   Heave away and don't you make a noise
   We are bound for Australia.

Sourwood Mountain

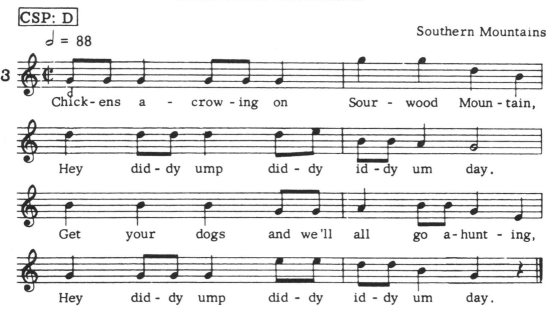

Southern Mountains

Chick-ens a - crow-ing on Sour - wood Moun-tain,

Hey did - dy ump did - dy id - dy um day.

Get your dogs and we'll all go a - hunt - ing,

Hey did - dy ump did - dy id - dy um day.

2. Raccoon canter and 'possum trot,
   Hey diddy ump diddy iddy um day.
   Black cur wrestle with a hickory knot,
   Hey diddy ump diddy iddy um day.

3. Bring your old dog, get your gun,
   Hey diddy ump diddy iddy um day.
   Kill some game and have a little fun,
   Hey diddy ump diddy iddy um day.

4. Jaybird sitting on a hickory limb,
   Hey diddy ump diddy iddy um day.
   My six-foot rifle will sure get him,
   Hey diddy ump diddy iddy um day.

5. Gather that game and at home I'll rack,
   Hey diddy ump diddy iddy um day.
   Got as much good meat as I can carry,
   Hey diddy ump diddy iddy um day.

6. I got a gal in the head of the hollow,
   Hey diddy ump diddy iddy um day.
   She won't come and I won't follow,
   Hey diddy ump diddy iddy um day.

7. She sits up with old Si Hall,
   Hey diddy ump diddy iddy um day.
   Me and Jeff can't go there at all,
   Hey diddy ump diddy iddy um day.

8. Some of these days before very long,
   Hey diddy ump diddy iddy um day.
   I'll get that girl and a-home I'll run,
   Hey diddy ump diddy iddy um day.

r d t, s,

Buy A Penny Ginger

CSP: G

Jamaican Game Song

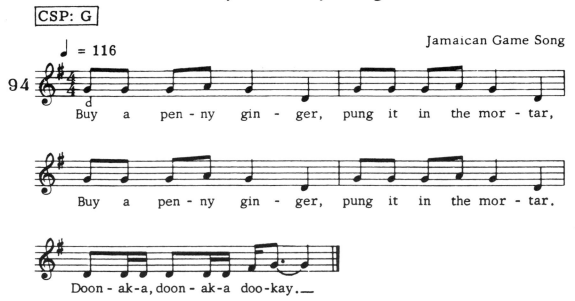

♩ = 116

94

Buy a pen-ny gin-ger, pung it in the mor-tar,

Buy a pen-ny gin-ger, pung it in the mor-tar.

Doon-ak-a, doon-ak-a doo-kay.

Game

Players stack hands over each other by pinching the back of each hand. The lowest hand rests on a table or on the ground. The higher the stack of hands the better. During the lines "Buy a penny ginger, Pung it in a mortar" which is chanted loudly by all players, the shoulders shrugged to give the stack of hands a slight upward and downward movement. During "Doonaka ..." the movement is accelerated. At "Dookay!" each hand is pulled away violently and pushed to the chest of the opposite player. The aim is to push the players down so that they fall in a heap. Players must regain their feet quickly and nimbly.

s f m r d

Aunt Rhody

CSP: F♯

♩ = 88

95

Go tell Aunt Rho - dy, Go tell Aunt Rho - dy,

Go tell Aunt Rho - dy, That the old gray goose is dead.

2. The one she's been saving,
The one she's been saving,
The one she's been saving,
To make a feather bed.

3. Old gander's weeping
Old gander's weeping
Old gander's weeping
Because his wife is dead.

4. And the goslings are mourning
And the goslings are mourning
And the goslings are mourning
Because their mother's dead.

5. She died in the millpond
She died in the millpond
She died in the millpond
Standing on her head.

The Deaf Woman's Courtship

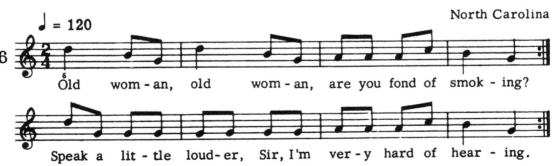

CSP: A

♩ = 120

North Carolina

96

Old wom - an, old wom - an, are you fond of smok - ing?

Speak a lit - tle loud - er, Sir, I'm ver - y hard of hear - ing.

2. Old woman, old woman, are you fond of carding?
Speak a little louder, Sir, I'm rather hard of hearing.

3. Old woman, old woman, don't you want me to court you?
Speak a little louder, Sir, I just began to hear you.

4. Old woman, old woman, don't you want to marry me?
Lord have mercy on my soul, I think that now I hear you.

68

Oats And Beans

CSP: A

Game Song

Oats and beans and bar-ley grow, oats and beans and bar-ley grow,

Do you or I or any-one know how oats and beans and bar-ley grow?

2. First the farmer sows his seed
   Then he stands and takes his ease
   Stamps his foot and claps his hands
   And turns around to view the land.

3. Waiting for a partner
   Waiting for a partner
   Break the ring and choose one in
   While all the others dance and sing.

4. Tra la la la la la la
   etc.

Game

Single circle, hands joined, one player in the center as Farmer. Circle walks to left while singing first stanza.

2nd stanza: Farmer goes through the action indicated by the words, the circle standing and doing the same.

3rd stanza: Circle moves to left while Farmer chooses a partner.

On the last stanza circle keeps to left, while Farmer and partner skip to right.

The partner so chosen becomes the Farmer when the game is repeated.

Let's Go To The Woods

New England

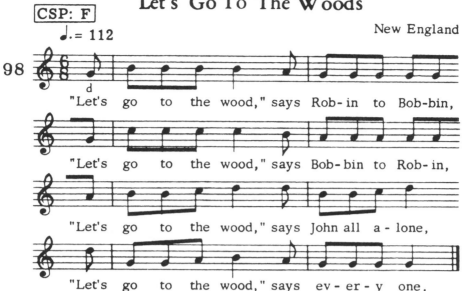

CSP: F

♩.= 112

98

"Let's go to the wood," says Rob-in to Bob-bin,

"Let's go to the wood," says Bob-bin to Rob-in,

"Let's go to the wood," says John all a-lone,

"Let's go to the wood," says ev-er-y one.

2. "Oh what to do there" says Robin to Bobbin,
"Oh what to do there" says Bobbin to Robin,
"Oh what to do there" says John all alone,
"Oh what to do there" says everyone.

3. "We'll scoot us a wren" says Robin to Bobbin,
"We'll scoot us a wren" says Bobbin to Robin,
"We'll scoot us a wren" says John all alone,
"We'll scoot us a wren" says everyone.

4. "How'll we get it home" says Robin to Bobbin,
"How'll we get it home" says Bobbin to Robin,
"How'll we get it home" says John all alone,
"How'll we get it home" says everyone.

5. "With a cart and six horses" says Robin to Bobbin,
"With a cart and six horses" says Bobbin to Robin,
"With a cart and six horses" says John all alone,
"With a cart and six horses" says everyone.

6. "Who will eat it" says Robin to Bobbin,
"Who will eat it" says Bobbin to Robin,
"Who will eat it" says John all alone,
"Who will eat it" says everyone.

7. "We'll all of us eat it" says Robin to Bobbin,
"We'll all of us eat it" says Bobbin to Robin,
"We'll all of us eat it" says John all alone,
"We'll all of us eat it" says everyone.

8. "What'll we do with the bones" says Robin to Bobbin,
"What'll we do with the bones" says Bobbin to Robin,
"What'll we do with the bones" says John all alone,
"What'll we do with the bones" says everyone.

9. "Leave the bones for the craws" says Robin to Bobbin,
"Leave the bones for the craws" says Bobbin to Robin,
"Leave the bones for the craws" says John all alone,
"Leave the bones for the craws" says everyone.

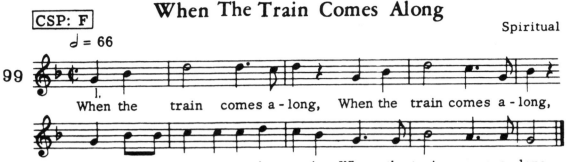

When The Train Comes Along

Spiritual

CSP: F

When the train comes a-long, When the train comes a-long, I'm going to meet you at the station, When the train comes a-long.

2. If my mother asks for me,
Tell her death done summon me,
I'm going to meet her at the station,
When the train comes along.

3. If my father asks for me,
Tell him death done summon me,
I'm going to meet her at the station,
When the train comes along.

4. If my brother asks for me,
Tell him death done summon me,
I'm going to meet her at the station,
When the train comes along.

Old Bald Eagle

Game Song

CSP: F

Old bald ea-gle sail a-round,
Day-light is gone;
Old bald ea-gle sail a-round,
Day-light is gone.

Old bald eagle sail around,
Daylight is gone;
Old bald eagle sail around,
Daylight is gone.

Backwards and forwards across the floor,
Daylight is gone,
Backwards and forwards across the floor,
Daylight is gone.

You swing here and I'll swing there,
Daylight is gone,
You swing here and I'll swing there,
Daylight is gone.

You go ride the old grey mare,
I'll go ride the roan,
If you get there before I do,
Leave my girl alone.

Sail around, Maggie, sail around,
Daylight is gone,
Sail around, Maggie, sail around,
Daylight is gone.

Big fine house in Baltimore,
Sixteen stories high,
Pretty little girl lives up there,
Hope she'll never die.

Old bald eagle sail around,
Daylight is gone;
Old bald eagle sail around,
Daylight is gone.

Game

The game is played with a large circle of children, with boys on the left side of their partners. The first couple joins hands and skips around inside the circle, back to their original place. The first couple then takes four steps towards the opposite couple, and as they take four steps back to place, the opposite couple takes four steps towards them and back to place. The first couple swing left arms, and then the boy in the first couple swings the girl in the second couple with his right arm, and then first couple swing each other with left again. They progress around the circle, the boy in the first couple swinging each girl with right arm and his partner with his left, while girl of first couple swings each boy with right arm and her partner with the left. This action is repeated with each couple in the circle leading.

72

d' t l s m

I'll Sell My Hat

CSP: D

♩ = 120

101

I'll sell my hat, I'll sell my coat,

To buy my wife a lit-tle flat boat.

Down the riv-er we will float,

Come bib-ble in the boo-shy-lo-ree.

Shule, shule, shule-i-rue,

Shule-i-rack-a-shak, shule-a-bar-be-que.

When I sell my Sal-ly bal-a-yeal,

Come bib-ble in the boo-shy-lo-ree.

2. I'll sell my pants, I'll sell my vest,
To get enough money to go out west,
And there I think I can do the best,
Come bibble in the booshyloree.
Shule, shule, shulerue,
Shuleirackashack, shuleabarbeque.
When I sell my Sally babayeal
Come bibble in the booshyloree.

Needle's Eye

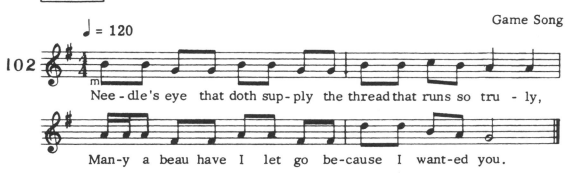

CSP: A

Game Song

♩ = 120

102

Nee - dle's eye that doth sup - ply the thread that runs so tru - ly,

Man-y a beau have I let go be - cause I want-ed you.

2. Mama taught me how to sew and how to thread the needle,
Every time my finger slips, pop goes the weasel.

Game

> The players hold hands to form an arch, others pass through —
> like in "London Bridge". At "pop goes . . ." arch drops hands to catch
> "thread". Player then chooses between the two sides — takes a place
> behind the leader. Game continues until all have been chosen.

Housekeeping

CSP: G♯

♩ = 126

103

Kit - tie put the ket - tle on, ket - tle on, ket - tle on,

Kit - tie put the ket - tle on, we'll all have tea.

Down To The Baker's Shop

CSP: D

Appalachian

104

♩ = 138

Down to the ba - ker's shop, hop hop hop!

For my moth - er said, "Buy a loaf of bread."

Down to the ba - ker's shop, hop hop hop!

London Bridge

CSP: A

Game Song

105

♩ = 112

Lon - don Bridge is fall - ing down, fall - ing down, fall - ing down,

Lon - don Bridge is fall - ing down, my fair— la - dy, O.

Off to pris - on you must go, you must go, you must go,

Off to pris - on you must go, my fair— la - dy, O.

2. Build it up with bricks and stones,
Bricks and stones, bricks and stones,
Build it up with bricks and stones,
My fair lady, O.
Bricks and stones will wash away,
Wash away, wash away,
Bricks and stones will wash away,
My fair lady, O.

I Love Little Willie

2. He wrote me a letter, he did, mama,
   He wrote me a letter, mama,
   He wrote me a letter but don't you tell Pa,
   'Cause he wouldn't like that, you know, mama.

3. He gave me a ring, he did, mama,
   He gave me a ring, mama,
   He gave me a ring but don't you tell Pa,
   'Cause he wouldn't like that, you know, mama.

4. We're going to get married, we are, mama,
   We're going to get married, mama,
   We're going to get married but don't you tell Pa,
   'Cause he wouldn't like that, you know, mama.

5. You must all come to see us, ha ha, mama,
   You must all come to see us, mama.
   You must all come to see us but don't you bring Pa,
   'Cause he wouldn't like it, you know, mama.

Alabama Gal

CSP: D ♩ = 112

107

Al - a - bam - a gal, won't you come out to - night,

Come out to - night, come out to - night.

Al - a - bam - a gal, won't you come out to - night,

And dance by the light of the moon.

This Lady

CSP: B ♩ = 168

Game Song

108

This la - dy she wears a dark green shawl,

A dark green shawl, a dark green shawl,

This la - dy she wears a dark green shawl,

I love her to my heart.

2. Now choose you a partner, honey my love,
Honey my love, honey my love.
Now choose you a partner, honey my love,
I love you to my heart.

3. Now dance with your partner, honey my love,
Honey my love, honey my love.
Now dance with your partner, honey my love,
I love you to my heart.

4. Farewell to your partner, honey my love,
Honey my love, honey my love.
Farewell to your partner, honey my love,
I love you to my heart.

3. Build it up with silver and gold,
   Silver and gold, silver and gold,
   Build it up with silver and gold,
   My fair lady, O.
   Thieves will steal the silver and gold,
   Silver and gold, silver and gold,
   Thieves will steal the silver and gold,
   My fair lady, O.

4. Build it up with iron bars
   Iron bars, iron bars,
   Build it up with iron bars,
   My fair lady, O.
   Iron bars will last for aye,
   Last for aye, last for aye,
   Iron bars will last for aye,
   My fair lady, O.

Game

Two players go away from the group secretly to choose bribes for their respective sides, such as a string of pearls for one side, a diamond necklace for the other. The bribes having been chosen, these two leaders return to the group and raise their clasped hands to form an arch. Then the group sings and marches through the arch. When the words "My fair lady, O" are sung, the leaders drop their arms quickly around the player just passing through, while everyone sings the chorus the prisoners are taken aside and offered their choices quietly. The prisoner then takes his place behind the leader whose gift he has selected. This goes on till all the players have chosen. A tug of war ends the game.

Around The Green Gravel

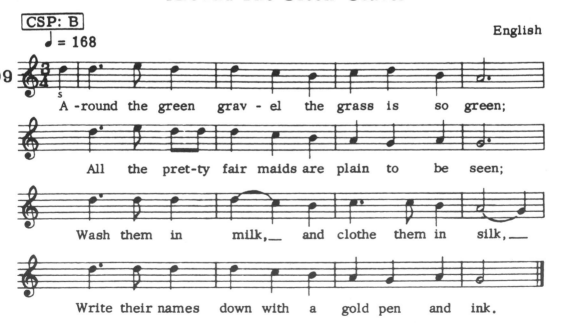

CSP: B
♩ = 168
English
109

A -round the green grav - el the grass is so green;

All the pret-ty fair maids are plain to be seen;

Wash them in milk,— and clothe them in silk,—

Write their names down with a gold pen and ink.

m r d t, l, s,

Give My Love To Nell

Alabama

CSP: D

♩ = 112

110

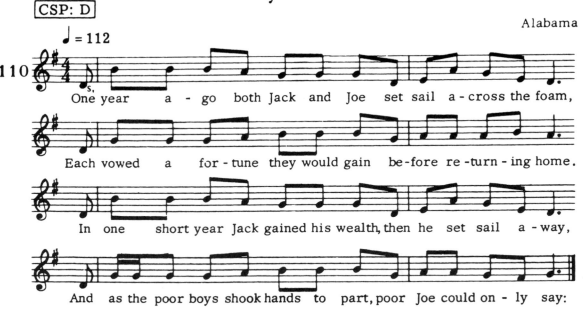

One year a - go both Jack and Joe set sail a - cross the foam,

Each vowed a for - tune they would gain be - fore re - turn - ing home.

In one short year Jack gained his wealth, then he set sail a - way,

And as the poor boys shook hands to part, poor Joe could on - ly say:

Chorus: *(to above melody)*

"Give my love to Nellie, Jack, and kiss her once for me
The fairest girl in all this world I know you'll say it's she,
Treat her kindly, Jack, I pray, and tell her that I am well
And when you've met, oh don't forget to give my love to Nell."

2. One year had passed when Joe at last has gained his wealth for life,
Then he set sail across the foam to make sweet Nell his wife.
But on his way he heard them say that Jack and Nell had wed:
Deeply he regretted then the words that he had said.

Chorus:

3. Upon the streets they chanced to meet. Said Joe, "You selfish elf,
The next girl I learn to love I'll kiss her for myself,
But all is fair in love and war and since you are wed
I'll not be angry with you, Jack," and once again he said:

Chorus:

"Give my love to Nellie, Jack, and kiss her once for me
The fairest girl in all this world I know you'll say it's she,
Treat her kindly, Jack, I pray, and tell her that I am well
And when you've met, oh don't forget to give my love to Nell."

All Around The Maypole

Afro-American Game Song

CSP: D

♩ = 104

11

All a-round the may-pole,

may-pole, may-pole,

All a-round the may-pole,

Now Miss Sal-ly won't you shout for joy?

Shout for joy, shout for joy,

shout for joy? (And)

Now Miss Sal-ly won't you shout for joy? (And)

Now Miss Sal-ly won't you bow?

Game

The players join hands in a ring and walk around, stopping and clapping hands while the player skipping in the center bows and chooses a partner to "jump" or dance with.

f m r d l, s,

Johnny Cuckoo

CSP: G

Afro-American

♩ = 96

112

Here come one John-ny Cuck-oo, Cuck - oo, cuck-oo,

Here come one John-ny Cuck-oo, On a cold and_storm-y night.

2. What did you come for,
   Come for, come for
   What did you come for
   On a cold and stormy night?

3. I come for many a soldier,
   Soldier, soldier,
   I come for many a soldier
   On a cold and stormy night.

4. You look too ragged and dirty,
   Dirty, dirty,
   You look too ragged and dirty
   On a cold and stormy night.

5. I'm just as clean as you are,
   You are, you are,
   I'm just as clean as you are
   On a cold and stormy night.

6. Here come two Johnny Cuckoo,
   Cuckoo, cuckoo,
   Here come two Johnny Cuckoo
   On a cold and stormy night.

7. What did you come for,
   Come for, come for,
   What did you come for
   On a cold and stormy night.

8. We come for us a soldier,
   A soldier, a soldier,
   We come for us a soldier
   On a cold and stormy night.

9. You look too ragged and dirty,
   Dirty, dirty,
   You look too ragged and dirty
   On a cold and stormy night.

10. We're just as clean as you are,
    You are, you are,
    We're just as clean as you are
    On a cold and stormy night.

13. We come for us a soldier,
    Soldier, soldier,
    We come for us a soldier
    On a cold and stormy night.

11. Here come three Johnny Cuckoo,
    Cuckoo, cuckoo,
    Here come three Johnny Cuckoo,
    On a cold and stormy night.

14. You look too ragged and dirty,
    Dirty, dirty,
    You look too ragged and dirty
    On a cold and stormy night.

12. What did you come for,
    Come for, come for,
    What did you come for
    On a cold and stormy night.

15. We're just as clean as you are,
    You are, you are,
    We're just as clean as you are
    On a cold and stormy night.

16. Here come four Johnny Cuckoo,
    Cuckoo, cuckoo,
    Here come four Johnny Cuckoo
    On a cold and stormy night.

Pharaoh's Army

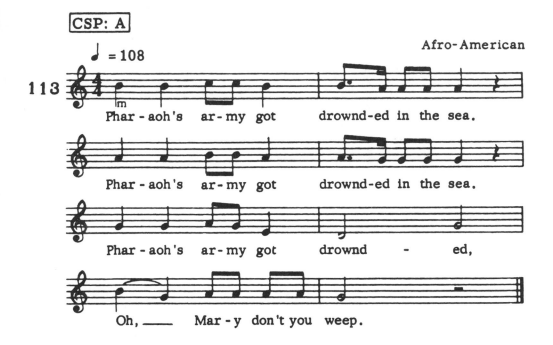

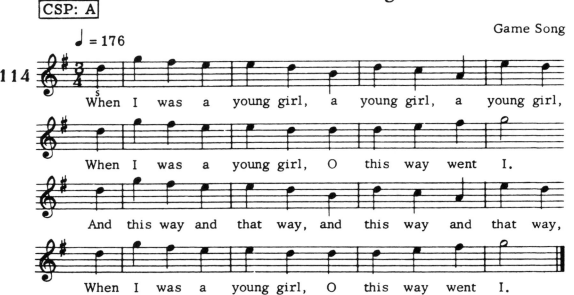

d' t l s f m r

When I Was A Young Girl

CSP: A

Game Song

♩ = 176

114

When I was a young girl, a young girl, a young girl,

When I was a young girl, O this way went I.

And this way and that way, and this way and that way,

When I was a young girl, O this way went I.

2. When I went acourting, acourting, acourting,
   When I went acourting, O this way went I.
   And this way and that way, and this way and that way.
   When I went acourting, O this way went I.

3. When I did get married, get married, get married,
   When I did get married, O this way went I.
   And this way and that way, and this way and that way.
   When I did get married, O this way went I.

4. When I had a baby, a baby, a baby,
   When I had a baby, how happy was I.
   And this way and that way, and this way and that way.
   When I had a baby, how happy was I.

5. When my husband was buried, was buried, was buried,
   When my husband was buried, how sorry was I.
   And this way and that way, and this way and that way.
   When my husband was buried, how sorry was I.

6. Then I took in washing, in washing, in washing,
   Then I took in washing, O this way went I.
   And this way and that way, and this way and that way.
   Then I took in washing, O this way went I.

7. Then I kept a pony, a pony, a pony,
   Then I kept a pony, O this way went I.
   And this way and that way, and this way and that way.
   Then I kept a pony, O this way went I.

Game

Players dance in ring during first two lines of each verse and perform the actions only on the last two lines. Actions for each verse can be agreed upon previously, or improvised for each verse by one player in the center of ring.

f m r d t, l, s,

The Three Rogues

Ohio

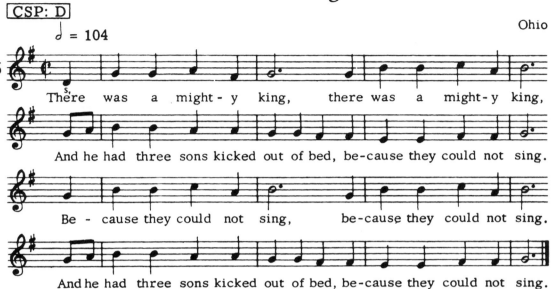

CSP: D

♩ = 104

15

There was a might-y king, there was a might-y king,

And he had three sons kicked out of bed, be-cause they could not sing.

Be - cause they could not sing, be-cause they could not sing.

And he had three sons kicked out of bed, be-cause they could not sing.

2. The first he was a miller,
   The second he was a weaver,
   And the third he was a little tailor boy
   With the broadcloth under his arm.
   With the broadcloth under his arm,
   With the broadcloth under his arm,
   And the third he was a little tailor boy
   With the broadcloth under his arm.

3. The miller he stole corn
   The weaver he stole yarn
   And the little tailor boy stole broadcloth enough
   To keep the three rogues warm.
   To keep the three rogues warm,
   To keep the three rogues warm,
   And the little tailor boy stole broadcloth enough,
   To keep the three rogues warm.

4. The miller got drowned in his dam,
   The weaver got hung in his yarn,
   And the devil caught the little tailor boy
   With the broadcloth under his arm.
   With the broadcloth under his arm,
   With the broadcloth under his arm,
   And the devil caught the little tailor boy,
   With the broadcloth under his arm.

d' s f m r d

Skipping Rope Song

Game Song

CSP: A

116 ♩ = 108

Early in the morning at eight o' clock,

you can hear the post-man's knock!

Up jump El - la to o-pen the door,

one letter, two letters, three letters, four.

Game

Girls holding the rope stamp their feet on the ground "Up jumps...",
girl named runs into the rope and begins to skip: "one letter,..." At the
last word she jumps out and takes one end of the rope and another runs
in, till each have had their turn.

Shoo My Love

North Carolina

CSP: C

117 ♩ = 108

Lei - la that's shoo my love, Lei - la that's shoo my love.

Turn me in a hur - ry now. Shoo Dol - ly, shoo my love,

Turn me in a hur - ry now. Shoo Dol - ly, shoo my love.

s f m r d s,

The Grand Old Duke Of York

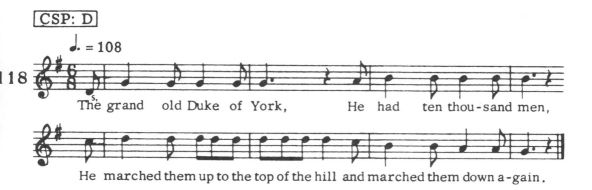

The grand old Duke of York, He had ten thou-sand men,

He marched them up to the top of the hill and marched them down a-gain.

> 2. And when they were up they were up
> And when they were down they were down
> And when they were only half way up
> They were neither up nor down.

Eency Weency Spider

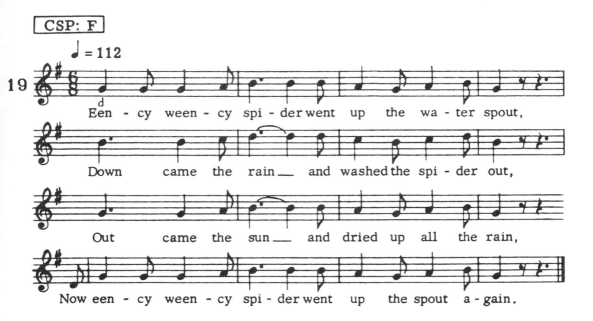

Een - cy ween - cy spi - der went up the wa - ter spout,

Down came the rain __ and washed the spi - der out,

Out came the sun __ and dried up all the rain,

Now een - cy ween - cy spi - der went up the spout a - gain.

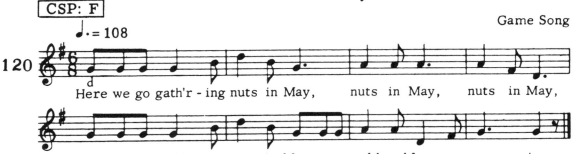

s m r d t, s,
Nuts In May

CSP: F

Game Song

♩.= 108

120

Here we go gath'r - ing nuts in May, nuts in May, nuts in May,

Here we go gath'r - ing nuts in May, on a cold and frost-y morn - ing.

Game

In England this is the most popular of all singing games. Mrs. Gomme shows that we ought to read "Knots of May" - i.e. bunches of the May or hawthorn; the maids are likened to such sprays, to be gathered by the lads and brought home as their "May". The manner of playing was probably the same as in Great Britain, where two children join hands and try to pull each other over a mark; the captured player joins the conqueror, and so until all are selected. Mrs. Gomme shows that boys were once chosen to bring in the girls, who were expected to resist.

d' t l s m r d
Johnny Has Gone For A Soldier

CSP: C

♩ = 104

121

Sad I sit on But-ter-nut Hill,

Who could blame me cry my fill?

And ev - 'ry tear would_ turn a mill,

John-ny has gone for a sol - dier.

2. Me o my, I loved him so.
   Broke my heart to see him go.
   And only time will heal my woe,
   Johnny has gone for a soldier.

3. I'd sell my clock, I'd sell my reel,
   Likewise I'd sell my spinning wheel,
   To buy my love a sword of steel
   Johnny has gone for a soldier.

* We have found no source that indicates the flatted seventh.
However, the song is traditionally sung with the F natural.

d' l s f m r d

Cripple Creek

CSP: C

♩ = 144

122

Go - ing up to Crip - ple Creek, go - ing on the run,

Go - ing up to Crip - ple Creek, to have some fun.

Tideo

CSP: F♯

Play-party Song

♩ = 108

123

Skip one win-dow, ti - de - o, Skip two win-dows, ti - de - o.

Skip three win-dows, ti - de - o. Jin-gle at the win-dows, ti - de - o.

Jin - gling, jin-gling, jin-gling Joe, Jin-gle at the win-dows, ti - de - o.

My Mammy Told Me

North Carolina

CSP: D

♩ = 120

24

My mam - my told me long years a - go,

"My son, don't you mar - ry no gal you know.

She'll spend all your mon - ey, wear out your clothes,

And what will be - come of you ___ the Lord on - ly knows".

88

l s f m r d l,

The Bell Cow

CSP: F

♩ = 144

125

Par-tridge in the pea-patch, pick-in' up the peas,

'Long come the bell cow, kick-in' up her heels!

Oh, the bell cow, ketch-'er by the tail,

Call the lit-tle gal to milk-'er in the pail!

s f m r d l, s,

Father Grumble

CSP: D

♩. = 108

New England

126

There was an old man that lived in a wood, as

you can plain-ly see, Who said he could do more

work in a day, than his wife could do in three.

"If that be so", the old wom-an said, "Why

this you must al-low, That you shall do my

work for a day, while I go drive the plough."

89

2. "But you must milk the tiny cow
For fear she should go dry
And you must feed the little pigs
That are within the sty,
And you must watch the bracket hen
Lest she should lay astray,
And you must wind the reel of yarn
That I spun yesterday."

3. The old woman took the staff in her hand
And went to drive the plough;
The old man took the pail in his hand
And went to milk the cow;
But Tiny hinched and Tiny flinched
And Tiny cocked her nose
And Tiny hit the old man such a kick
That the blood ran down to his toes.

4. 'T'was, "Hey my good cow," and "How, my good cow,"
And "Now my good cow, stand still.
If ever I milk this cow again,
'Twill be against my will."
And when he'd milked the tiny cow
For fear she should go dry,
Why, then he fed the little pigs
That were within the sty.

5. And then he watched the bracket hen,
Lest she should lay astray,
But he forgot the reel of yarn
His wife spun yesterday.
He swore by all the leaves on the tree,
And all the stars in heaven,
That his wife could do more work in a day
Than he could do in seven.

Taken from Eloise Linscott's "Songs of North America."
Used by permission of The Shoestring Press, Inc.

90

sfmrdt,s,

Down In The Valley

CSP: D

Kentucky

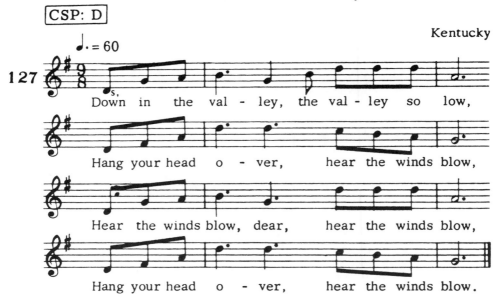

127

♩.= 60

Down in the val - ley, the val - ley so low,

Hang your head o - ver, hear the winds blow,

Hear the winds blow, dear, hear the winds blow,

Hang your head o - ver, hear the winds blow.

2. If you don't love me, love whom you please,
Throw your arms 'round me, give my heart ease,
Give my heart ease, dear, give my heart ease,
Throw your arms 'round me, give my heart ease.

3. Throw your arms 'round me, before it's too late,
Throw your arms 'round me, feel my heart break.
Feel my heart break, dear, feel my heart break,
Throw your arms 'round me, feel my heart break.

4. If you don't love me, none else will do,
My heart is breaking, dear, just for you.
Breaking for you, dear, breaking for you,
My heart is breaking, dear, just for you.

5. Writing this letter, containing three lines,
Answer my question: Will you be mine?
Will you be mine, dear, will you be mine,
Answer my question: Will you be mine?

6. Build me a castle forty feet high,
So's I can see him as he goes by.
As he goes by, dear, as he goes by,
So's I can see him as he goes by.

7. Down in the valley, the mocking bird wings,
Telling my story, here's what he sings:
Roses love sunshine, violets love dew,
Angels in heaven knows I love you.

8. Knows I love you, dear, knows I love you,
Angels in heaven knows I love you.
Knows I love you, dear, knows I love you,
Angels in heaven knows I love you.

s m r d t, l, s,

Watch That Lady

CSP: F

♩ = 100

Afro-American Game Song

128

(I) Been all a-round my last___ time,

last___ time, last___ time,

(I) Been all a-round my last___ time,

Young la - dy, hold the key.

First watch that la-dy how she hold that key,

Young la - dy hold the key.

Directions

This is played as a ring game with one child in the center of the circle pretending to "hold that key". All of the children sing. The one in the center makes various motions, such as combing her hair, kneeling, standing on one foot, or shaking her body, and those in the circle try to imitate her.

In this recording the children clap their hands. Other groups playing the same game sometimes hold their hands on their hips instead of clapping. Forms of this game are found in the West Indian islands of Jamaica, Trinidad and Martinique. In Haiti the game is known as "Theatre".

d' t l s f m r d

The Little Dappled Cow

CSP: A

♩ = 100

129

Once there was a lit - tle man, where the lit-tle riv - er ran,

And he had a lit - tle farm and lit - tle dai - ry - o.

And he had a lit - tle plow, and a lit-tle dap-pled cow,

Which he oft-en called his pret - ty lit - tle Mar - y - o.

2. Then his little maiden ran with her pretty little can
   Went a-milking when the morning-sun was beaming-o,
   And she fell on the cow, and she stumbled o'er the plow,
   And the cow was quite astonished at her streaming-o.

3. Little maid 'twere all in vain, as the milk ran o'er the plain,
   And the piggy went a-grunting oh so gaily-o,
   And the little dog behind thought his share was much inclined
   So he pulled that squealing piggy by the taily-o.

4. Then to make a story short, little pony with a snort,
   Lifting up his little heels so clever-o,
   And the man he tumbled down, and he nearly cracked his crown,
   And this only made the matter worse than ever-o.

Sweet Betsy From Pike

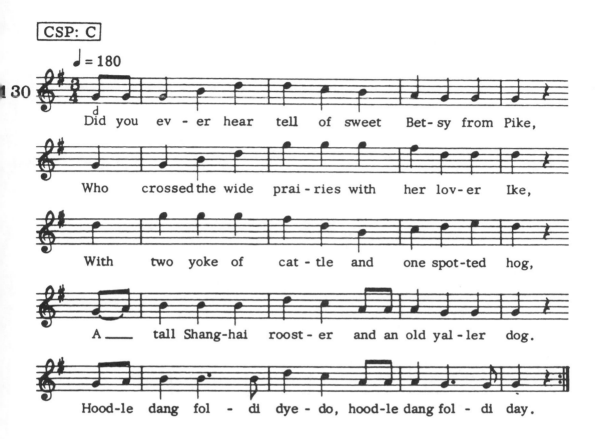

CSP: C

♩ = 180

130

Did you ev - er hear tell of sweet Bet- sy from Pike,

Who crossed the wide prai - ries with her lov- er Ike,

With two yoke of cat - tle and one spot-ted hog,

A ___ tall Shang-hai roost - er and an old yal - ler dog.

Hood-le dang fol - di dye - do, hood-le dang fol - di day.

Refrain: Hoo-dle dang fol-di dye-do, hoo-dle dang fol-di day,
Hoo-dle dang fol-di dye-do, hoo-dle dang fol-di day.

2. One evening quite early they camped on the Platte,
Made down their blankets on a green shady flat;
Where Betsy, quite tired, lay down to repose,
While with wonder Ike gazed on his Pike County road.

3. They swam the wide rivers and crossed the tall peaks,
And camped on the prairie for weeks upon weeks.
Starvation and cholera and hard work and slaughter,
They reached California spite of hell and high water.

4. Out on the prairie one bright starry night
They broke out the whisky and Betsy got tight;
She sang and she shouted and danced o'er the plain,
And made a great show for the whole wagon train.

5. The Injuns came down in a wild yelling horde,
And Betsy was skeered they would scalp her adored;
Behind the front wagon wheel Betsy did crawl,
And fought off the Injuns with musket and ball.

6. They soon reached the desert, where Betsy gave out,
And down in the sand she lay rolling about;
While Ike in great terror looked on in surprise,
Saying, "Get up now, Betsy, you'll get sand in your eyes."

7. The wagon tipped over with a terrible crash,
And out on the prairie rolled all sort of trash;
A few little baby clothes done up with care
Looked rather suspicious — though 'twas all on the square.

8. The Shanghai ran off and the cattle all died,
The last piece of bacon that morning was fried;
Poor Ike got discouraged, and Betsy got mad,
The dog wagged his tail and looked wonderfully sad.

9. One morning they climbed up a very high hill,
And with wonder looked down into old Placerville;
Ike shouted and said, as he cast his eyes down,
"Sweet Betsy, my darling, we've got to Hangtown."

10. Long Ike and sweet Betsy attended a dance,
Where Ike wore a pair of his Pike County pants;
Sweet Betsy was covered with ribbons and rings.
Said Ike, "You're an angel, but where are your wings?"

11. A miner said, "Betsy, will you dance with me?"
"I will that, old hoss, if you don't make too free;
But don't dance me hard. Do you want to know why?
Doggone you, I'm chock-full of strong alkali."

12. Long Ike and sweet Betsy got married of course,
But Ike, getting jealous, obtained a divorce;
And Betsy, well satisfied, said with a shout,
"Good-by, you big lummux, I'm glad you backed out."

Final Chorus: Saying, good-by, dear Isaac,
Farewell for a while,
But come back in time
To replenish my pile.

$\boxed{\text{s f m r d t, l, s,}}$

Pick A Bale Of Cotton

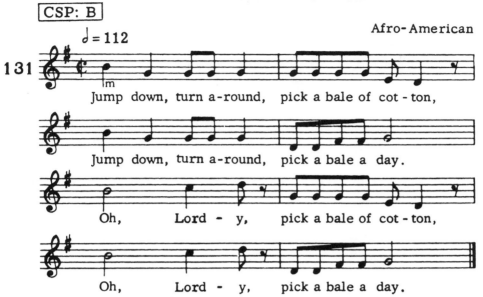

Afro-American

CSP: B

131

Jump down, turn a-round, pick a bale of cot-ton,

Jump down, turn a-round, pick a bale a day.

Oh, Lord - y, pick a bale of cot-ton,

Oh, Lord - y, pick a bale a day.

Hushabye

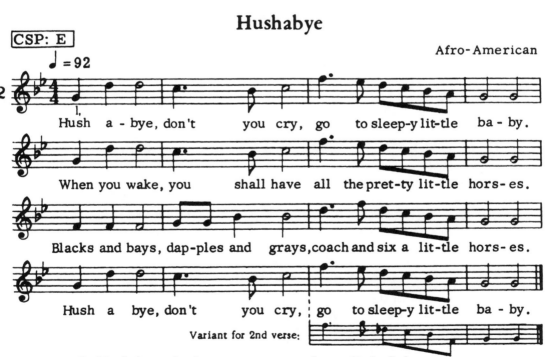

Afro-American

CSP: E

132

Hush a - bye, don't you cry, go to sleep-y lit-tle ba - by.

When you wake, you shall have all the pret-ty lit-tle hors-es.

Blacks and bays, dap-ples and grays, coach and six a lit-tle hors-es.

Hush a bye, don't you cry, go to sleep-y lit-tle ba - by.

Variant for 2nd verse:

2. Hushabye, don't you cry, go to sleepy little baby.
Way down yonder in the meadow lies a poor little lamb.
The bees and butterflies picking out its eyes,
poor little thing cries "Mammy".
Hushabye, don't you cry, go to sleepy little baby.

The Sailor's Alphabet

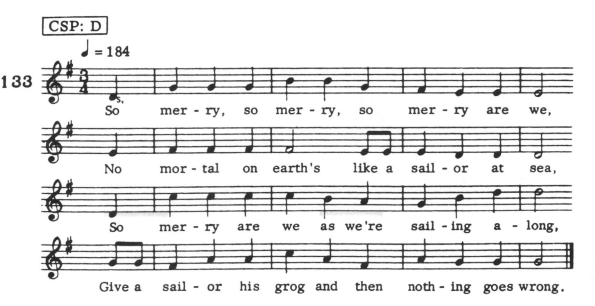

CSP: D

𝅘𝅥 = 184

133

So mer - ry, so mer - ry, so mer - ry are we,

No mor - tal on earth's like a sail - or at sea,

So mer - ry are we as we're sail - ing a - long,

Give a sail - or his grog and then noth - ing goes wrong.

2. Oh, A is the anchor and that you all know,
   B is the bowsprit that's over the bow
   C is the capstan with which we heave 'round
   And D are the decks where our sailors are found.

3. O, E is the ensign our mizzen-peak flew,
   F is the co'c'sle where we muster our crew,
   G are the guns, sir, by which we all stand,
   And H are the halyards that oft'times are manned.

4. Oh, I is the iron of our stunsail boom sheet,
   J is the jib that oft weathers the bleat,
   K is the keelson away down below,
   And L are the lanyards that give us good hold.

5. M is our mainmast so stout and so strong,
   N is the needle that never points wrong,
   O are the oars of our jollyboat's crew,
   And P is the pennant of red, white, and blue.

6. Q is the quarterdeck where our captain oft stood,
   R is the rigging that ever holds good,
   S are the stilliards that weigh out our beef,
   And T are the topsails we oft'times do reef.

7. Oh, U is the Union at which none dare laugh,
   V are the vangs that steady the gaff,
   W's the wheel that we all take in time,
   And X is the letter for which we've no rhyme.

8. Oh, Y are the yards that we oft'times do brace,
   Z is the letter for which we've no place,
   The bo'sun pipes grog, so we'll all go below,
   My song it is finished, I'm glad that it's so.

d' l s f m r d t,

There's A Brown Girl

Jamaican Game Song

♩ = 144

134

There's a brown girl in the ring, tra-la-la-la-la,

There's a brown girl in the ring, tra-la-la-la-la,

There's a brown girl in the ring, tra-la-la-la-la,

For she like sug-ar and I like plum.

2. Then you show me your motion, tra-la-la-la-la,
Then you show me your motion, tra-la-la-la-la;
Then you show me your motion, tra-la-la-la-la,
For she like sugar and I like plum.

3. Then you skip across the ocean, tra-la-la-la-la,
Then you skip across the ocean, tra-la-la-la-la,
Then you skip across the ocean, tra-la-la-la-la,
For she like sugar and I like plum.

4. Then you wheel and take your partner, tra-la-la-la-la,
Then you wheel and take your partner, tra-la-la-la-la,
Then you wheel and take your partner, tra-la-la-la-la,
For she like sugar and I like plum.

5. Then you stand and face your lover, tra-la-la-la-la,
Then you stand and face your lover, tra-la-la-la-la,
Then you stand and face your lover, tra-la-la-la-la,
For she like sugar and I like plum.

6. There's a brown girl in the ring, tra-la-la-la-la,
There's a brown girl in the ring, tra-la-la-la-la,
There's a brown girl in the ring, tra-la-la-la-la,
For she like sugar and I like plum.

Game

All players except one in the center who is the brown girl join hands to form a circle. They sing "There's a brown girl in the ring, etc." At the second verse "Show me your motion," the one in the circle moves her body in any way she chooses to the rhythm of the song. At the third verse "Skip across the ocean," brown girl skips toward one end of the circle and back. At the fourth verse "Wheel and take your partner," the one in the circle chooses one from the ring as her partner and they dance together in the center. Then they change places and the partner becomes the brown girl. The object of each player is to show his prowess as a dancer in the ring.

l s f m r d s,

Looby Loo

Game Song

CSP: F

135

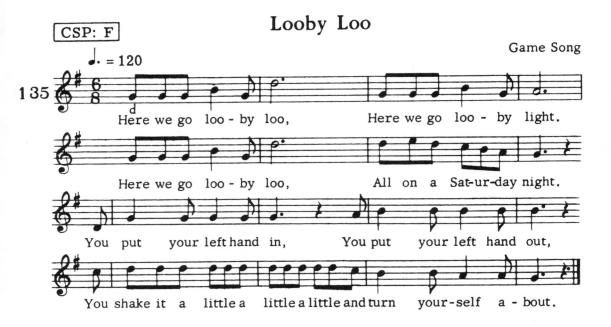

Here we go loo - by loo,   Here we go loo - by light.

Here we go loo - by loo,   All on a Sat-ur-day night.

You put   your left hand in,   You put   your left hand out,

You shake it a   little a   little a little and turn   your-self   a - bout.

2. Here we go looby loo
   Here we go looby light
   Here we go looby loo
   All on a Saturday night.
   You put your right hand in
   You put your right hand out
   You shake it a little, a little, a little
   And turn yourself about.

3. Here we go looby loo
   Here we go looby light
   Here we go looby loo
   All on a Saturday night.
   You put your left leg in
   You put your left leg out
   You shake it a little, a little, a little
   And turn yourself about.

4. Here we go looby loo
   Here we go looby light
   Here we go looby loo
   All on a Saturday night
   You put your right leg in
   You put your right leg out
   You shake it a little, a little, a little
   And turn yourself about.

5. Here we go looby loo
   Here we go looby light
   Here we go looby loo
   All on a Saturday night
   You put your whole self in,
   You put your whole self out,
   You shake it a little, a little, a little
   And turn yourself about.

Game

Children stand in a circle, and follow
the activities of the verses of the song.

May Day Carol

CSP: A   Kentucky

♩ = 104

136

I've been a wan - d'ring_ all the_ night,

And the best part of _ the day,

Now I'm re - turn - ing_ home a - gain,

I bring you a branch of_ May.

2. A branch of May, my love, I say,
   Here at your door I stand.
   It's nothing but a sprout, but it's well budded out
   By the work of the Lord's own hand.

3. Take a Bible in your hand
   And read a chapter through,
   And when the day of judgment comes,
   The Lord will think of you.

4. In my pocket I've got a purse
   Tied up with a silver string.
   All that I do need is a bit of silver
   To line it well within.

Blow, Boys, Blow

Sea Chantey

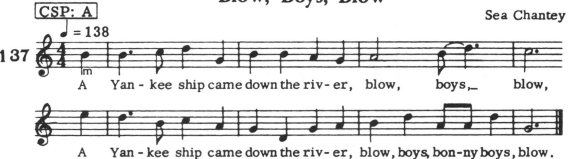

A Yan-kee ship came down the riv-er, blow, boys,— blow,

A Yan-kee ship came down the riv-er, blow, boys, bon-ny boys, blow.

2. And how do you know she's a Yankee clipper?
Blow, boys, blow,
Oh, how do you know she's a Yankee clipper?
Blow, boys, bonny, boys, blow.

3. The stars and bars they flew behind her,
Blow, boys, blow,
The stars and bars they flew behind her.
Blow, boys, bonny, boys, blow.

4. And who do you think was the skipper of her?
Blow, boys, blow,
A blue-nosed Nova Scotia hardcase.
Blow, boys, bonny, boys, blow.

5. And who do you think was the chief mate of her?
Blow, boys, blow,
A loud-mouthed disbarred Boston lawyer.
Blow, boys, bonny, boys, blow.

6. And what do you think we had for breakfast?
Blow, boys, blow.
The starboard side of an old sou'wester.
Blow, boys, bonny, boys, blow.

7. Then what do you think we had for dinner?
Blow, boys, blow.
We had monkey's heart and shark's liver.
Blow, boys, bonny, boys, blow.

8. Can you guess what we had for supper?
Blow, boys, blow.
We had strong salt junk and weak tea water.
Blow, boys, bonny, boys, blow.

9. Then blow us out and blow us homeward,
Blow, boys, blow.
Oh, blow today and blow tomorrow.
Blow, boys, bonny, boys, blow.

10. Blow fair and steady, mild and pleasant,
Blow, boys, blow,
Oh, blow us into Boston Harbor.
Blow, boys, bonny, boys, blow.

11. We'll blow until our blow is over.
Blow, boys, blow,
From Singapore to Cliffs of Dover,
Blow, boys, bonny, boys, blow.

t l s f m r d l₁

The Raggle Taggle Gypsies

CSP: A

♩ = 136

West Virginia

138

Last __ night three gyp - sies __ came to my door,

And down the stairs ran my La - dy, O.

And one sang high and one __ sang low,

And one sang "Bon - nie, Bon - nie, Bis - ca, O".

2. Then she stripped off her silk-finished gown
   And put on hose of leather, O!
   And ragged, ragged rags around the door,
   She's off with the raggle taggle gypsies, O!

*Sweet William

CSP: D

♩ = 112

39

Fa - ther, fa - ther build me a boat, that

on the o - cean I may float.

Light is the col-or of my true love's hair, his

cheeks re - sem - ble some la - dies fair.

Fa - ther, fa - ther build me a boat, that

on the o - cean I may float.

l s f m r d t, s,

The Paw-Paw Patch

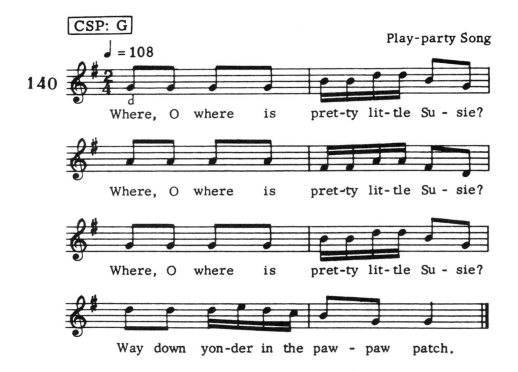

CSP: G

♩ = 108

Play-party Song

140

Where, O where is pret-ty lit-tle Su - sie?

Where, O where is pret-ty lit-tle Su - sie?

Where, O where is pret-ty lit- tle Su - sie?

Way down yon-der in the paw - paw patch.

2. Pickin' up paw-paws, puttin' um in her pockets,
   Pickin' up paw-paws, puttin' um in her pockets,
   Pickin' up paw-paws, puttin' um in her pockets,
   Way down yonder in the paw-paw patch.

3. Come on boys, let's go find her,
   Come on boys, let's go find her,
   Come on boys, let's go find her,
   Way down yonder in the paw-paw patch.

Old Molly Hare (Mr. Rabbit)

Ole Mol - ly Hare, what you do - in' there?

Run - nin' through the cot - ton patch hard as I can tear.

Ole Mol - ly Hare, what you do - in' there?

Run - nin' through the cot - ton patch hard as I can tear.

Shack a lack a shack a lack a shack a lack a shay.

Shack a lack a shack a lack a shack a lack a shay.

l s f m r d t, l, s,

Goodbye Girls, I'm Going To Boston

CSP: D

♩=96

142

Good - bye girls, I'm going to Bos - ton,

Good - bye girls, I'm going to Bos-ton.

Good bye girls, I'm going to Bos - ton

ear - ly in the morn - ing.

Won't we look pret-ty in the ball - room?

Won't we look pret-ty in the ball - room?

Won't we look pret-ty in the ball - room

ear - ly in the morn - ing?

Poor Rosy

Afro-American

Poor Ro-sy, poor_ gal, poor Ro-sy, poor__ gal, Ro-sy break my poor heart, Heav'n shall a be my home.

Cradle Hymn

Hush, my babe, lie still and slum-ber
Ho - ly an - gels guard thy bed.
Heav'n-ly bless-ings with-out_ num - ber
Gent - ly steal-ing on thy head.

2. How much better art thou attended
   Than the Son of God could be
   When from heaven he descended
   And became a child like thee.

3. Soft and easy is thy cradle,
   Coarse and hard the Savior lay
   When His birthplace was a stable
   And His softest bed was hay.

Santy Anna

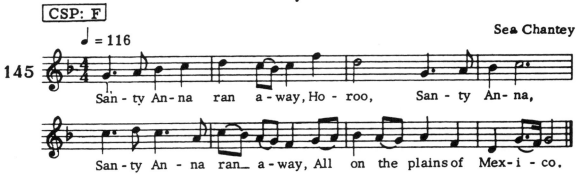

l m r d t, l, s, m,

Poor Little Jesus

2. It was poor little Jesus, Yes, yes,
   Child of Mary, Yes, yes,
   He was laid in a manger, Yes, yes,
   Wasn't that a pity and a shame, oh Lord,
   Wasn't that a pity and a shame.

1st half: m' r' d' t l s m

2nd half [l = d]: l s f m r d

My Old Hen

CSP: D

♩ = 80

147

My old hen's a good old hen, She lays eggs for the

rail - road men.

Some-times one, some - times two, Some-times e-nough for the

whole blamed crew.

Cluck, old hen, cluck, I tell you Cluck old hen, or

I'm a-going to sell you,

Cluck, old hen, cluck, I say Cluck old hen, or I'll

give you a-way.

d' t_a l s m r d

I'm Goin' Home On A Cloud

CSP: A

Afro-American

148

♩ = 80

One of these fine morn - ings at break of day,

I'm go - ing home on a cloud._____

King Death going to find me here at my play,

I'm go - ing home _ on _ a cloud. _____

2. If you don't ever, ever see me again
I'm going home on a cloud.
I'm going to hail the morning train,
I'm going home on a cloud.

3. I'm a poor pilgrim journeying alone,
I'm going home on a cloud.
Going to walk with the angels and sing around the throne.
I'm going home on a cloud.

4. O my Redeemer, Father of all
I'm going home on a cloud.
Here stands a soldier waiting for the call
I'm going home on a cloud.

t a l s f m r d s,

Old Joe Clarke

CSP: F

149 ♩ = 132

Round and round, old Joe Clark, Round and round, I say

Fine

Round and round, old Joe Clark, I ain't got long to stay.

Old Joe Clark, he had a house, Six-teen sto-ries high.

D. C. al Fine

Ev-'ry sto-ry in that house was full of chick-en pie.

OTHER REFRAINS:

Rock-a-rock, old Joe Clarke,
Rock-a-rock, I'm gone;
Rock-a-rock, old Joe Clarke,
And goodbye, Susan Brown.

Fly around, old Joe Clarke,
Fly around, I'm gone;
Fly around, old Joe Clarke,
With the golden slippers on.

Row around, old Joe Clarke,
Sail away and gone;
Row around, old Joe Clarke,
With golden slippers on.

Roll, roll, old Joe Clarke,
Roll, roll, I say;
Roll, roll, old Joe Clarke,
You'd better be gettin' away.

OTHER STANZAS:

Old Joe Clarke he had a dog
As blind as he could be;
Chased a redbug 'round a stump
And a coon up a hollow tree.

I went down to old Joe's house,
Never been there before,
He slept on the feather bed
And I slept on the floor.

If you see that girl of mine,
Tell her if you can,
Before she goes to make up bread
To wash those dirty hands.

When I was a little boy
I used to play in ashes.
Now I am a great big boy
Wearing Dad's mustaches.

s₁ m r d t₁ l₁ s₁ m₁

The Grey Goose

CSP: E

Afro-American

150

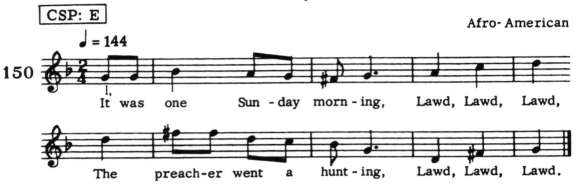

It was one Sun-day morn-ing, Lawd, Lawd, Lawd,

The preach-er went a hunt-ing, Lawd, Lawd, Lawd.

2. He carried 'long his shotgun,
Lawd, Lawd, Lawd,
When along came a grey goose,
Lawd, Lawd, Lawd.

3. The gun went off "Booloo",
Lawd, Lawd, Lawd.
And down came the grey goose,
Lawd, Lawd, Lawd.

4. He was six weeks a-fallin',
Lawd, Lawd, Lawd,
He was six weeks a-fallin',
Lawd, Lawd, Lawd.

5. And my wife and your wife,
Lawd, Lawd, Lawd,
They give a feather pickin',
Lawd, Lawd, Lawd.

6. They were six weeks a-pickin',
Lawd, Lawd, Lawd,
And they put him on to par-boil,
Lawd, Lawd, Lawd.

7. He was six weeks a-boilin',
Lawd, Lawd, Lawd,
And they put him on the table,
Lawd, Lawd, Lawd.

8. Well, the knife wouldn't cut him,
Lawd, Lawd, Lawd,
And the fork wouldn't stick him,
Lawd, Lawd, Lawd.

9. They put him in the hog pen,
Lawd, Lawd, Lawd,
And he broke the hog's teeth out,
Lawd, Lawd, Lawd.

10. They take him to the saw mill,
Lawd, Lawd, Lawd,
And the saw couldn't cut him,
Lawd, Lawd, Lawd.

11. And the last time I *seed him,
Lawd, Lawd, Lawd,
He was flyin' 'cross the ocean,
Lawd, Lawd, Lawd.

12. With a long string of goslings,
Lawd, Lawd, Lawd,
And they all goin' "Quank, Quank".
Lawd, Lawd, Lawd.

INDEX OF FIRST LINES

111

112

BIBLIOGRAPHY

Armitage, Theresa, *Our First Music*, C. C. Birchard and Co., Boston, 1941.

Arnold, Byron, collector, *Folksongs of Alabama*, University of Alabama Press, Birmingham, 1950.

Asch, Moses, *104 Folk Songs*, Robbins Music Corp., N.Y. 1964.

Beckwith, Martha W., *Folk Games of Jamaica*, Folklore Publications, Vassar College, 1922.

Botkin, Benjamin, *The American Play Party Song*, Nebraska University Press, Lincoln, 1937.

Broadwood, Lucy E., *English Country Songs*, Boosey & Company, London, 1893.

Brown, Florence W. and Neva L. Boyd, *Old English and American Games for School and Playground*, Soul Brothers, Chicago, 1915.

Brown, Frank C., *North Carolina Folklore*, Duke University Press, Durham, N.C., 1962.

Burlin, Natalie C., *Negro Folk-Songs*, Schirmer, Inc., New York, 1918.

Chase, Richard, *American Folk Tales and Songs*, Dover Publ., N.Y., 1971.

Colcord, Joanna, *Songs of American Sailormen*, Oak Publications, New York, 1964.

Courlander, Harold, *Negro Folk Music USA*, Columbia University Press, New York, 1963.

Courlander, Harold, *Negro Songs from Alabama*, Oak Publications, New York, 1963.

Cox, John Harrington, *Traditional Ballads, Mainly from West Virginia*, National Service Bureau, New York, 1939.

Dallin, Leon and Lynn, *Heritage Songster*, W. C. Brown Company Publishers, Dubuque, Iowa, 1966.

Dykema, Peter, *Twice 55 Games with Music*, Birchard & Company, Boston, 1924.

Eddy, Mary O., *Ballads and Songs from Ohio*, Folklore Associates, Inc., Hatboro, Pennsylvania, 1964.

Elder, David Paul, *Song Games from Trinidad and Tobago*, Publication of the American Folklore Society, 1965.

Farnsworth, Charles H. and Cecil F. Sharp, *Folk-Songs, Chanteys and Singing Games*, H. W. Gray Company, New York, 1916.

Foreman, *High Road of Song*, 1931.

Fowke, Edith, *Sally Go Round the Sun*, Doubleday, Garden City, New York, 1969.

Gillington, Alice E., *Old Surrey Singing Games*, J. Curwen & Sons, Ltd., London, 1909.

Gomme, Alice B. and Cecil F. Sharp, *Children's Singing Games*, Section II, Novello & Company, Ltd., London, 1909.

Gordon, Dorothy, *Sing It Yourself*, E. P. Dutton and Company, New York, 1928.

Hudson, Florence, *Songs of the Americas*, G. Schirmer, Inc., New York, 1922.

Johnson, Guy B., *Folk Culture on St. Helena Island*, South Carolina; Folklore Associates Inc., Hatboro, Pa., 1968.

Katz, Fred, *The Social Implications of Early Negro Music in the U.S.*, Arno Press, New York Times, 1969.

Kennedy, Robert E., *Black Cameos*, Albert & C. Boni, New York, 1924.

Kersey, Robert E., *Just Five – A Collection of Pentatonic Songs*, The Westminster Press, Maryland, 1970.

Kolb, Sylvia and John, *A Treasury of Folk Song*, Bantam Books, New York, 1948.

Landeck, Beatrice, *Songs to Grow On*, Edward B. Marks Music Company, Music Publishers, New York, 1950.

Linscott, Eloise Hubbard, *Folk Songs of Old New England*, Archon Books, Hamden, Conn., 1962.

Lomax, Alan, *Folk Songs of North America*, Doubleday and Company, New York, 1960.

Lomax, Alan and John, *Our Singing Country*, MacMillan Company, New York, 1941.

Lomax, John and Alan, *Folk Song U.S.A.*, Duell, Sloan and Pearce, Inc., New York, 1948.

Lomax, John and Alan, *Folk Song U.S.A.*, Meredith Press, New York, 1968.

Matteson, Maurice, *American Folksongs for Young Singers*, G. Schirmer, Inc., New York, 1947.

McIntosh, David, *Singing Games and Dances*, Association Press, New York, 1957.

Moses, Irene E. P., *Rhythmic Action, Plays and Dances*, Milton Bradley & Company, Springfield, Mass., 1915.

Newell, William W., *Games and Songs of American Children*, Dover Publications, New York, 1963.

Owens, William A., *Swing and Turn: Texas Playparty Games*, Tardy Publications Company, Dallas, Texas, 1936.

Porter, Grace Cleveland, *Negro Folk Singing Games and Folk Games of the Habitants*, J. Curwen and Sons, Ltd., London, 1914.

Randolph, Vance, *Ozark Folksongs*, The State Historical Society of Missouri, Columbia, Missouri, 1949.

Richardson, Ethel Park, *American Mountain Songs*, Greenberg Publisher, New York, 1927.

Ritchie, Jean T. R., *Golden City*, Oliver A. Boyd, Edinborough-London, 1965.

Ritchie, Jean T. R., *Singing Family of the Cumberlands*, Oxford University Press, New York, 1955.

Scarborough, Dorothy, *On the Trail of Negro Folksongs*, Folklore Association, Inc., Hatboro, Pa., 1963.

Seeger, Pete, *American Favorite Ballads*, Oak Publications, New York, 1961.

Seeger, Ruth Crawford, *Animal Folksongs for Children*, Doubleday and Company, Inc., Garden City, New York, 1950.

Seeger, Ruth Crawford, *American Folksongs for Children*, Doubleday and Company, Garden City, New York, 1948.

Seeger, Ruth Crawford, *American Folksongs for Children*, Doubleday and Company, Garden City, New York, 1953.

Sharp, Cecil, *English Folksongs from the Southern Appalachians*, Oxford University Press, London, 1966.

Sharp, Cecil, *Twelve Songs for Children from the Appalachian Mountains*, Oxford University Press, London, 1945.

Thomas, Jean and Joseph A. Leeder, *The Singin' Gatherin'*, Silver Burdett Company, 1939.

Tobitt, Janet Evelyn, *A Book of Negro Songs*, copyright by J. E. Tobitt, Pleasantville, New York, 1950.

Trent-Johns, Altona, *Play Songs of the Deep South*, The Associated Publishers, Inc., Washington, D. C., 1945.

Walter, Lavinia Edna, *Old English Singing Games*, A. & C. Black, Ltd., London, 1926.

Weavers Songbook, The, Harper & Brothers, New York, 1960.

White, Newman Ivey, *American Negro Folk Songs*, Folklore Associates, Hatboro, Pennsylvania, 1965.

PERIODICALS

Journal of American Folklore, Vol. 24, 1937.
  Missouri Play Party, by L. D. Ames.

Journal of American Folklore, Vol. 45, 1932.
  Still More Ballads and Folk-Songs from the Southern Highlands, by Mellinger E. Henry.

Journal of American Folklore, Vol. 49, 1936.
  Songs of the Cumberlands, by Bess A. Owens.

DISCOGRAPHY

1. *Afro-American Blues and Game Songs,* Library of Congress, Recording Laboratory, AFS L4.
2. *American Folksongs for Children,* Southern Folk Heritage Series, Atlantic, SD 1350.
3. *American Sea Songs and Chanties* (1), Library of Congress, Recording Laboratory, AAFS L26.
4. *Anglo-American Songs and Ballads,* Library of Congress, Recording Laboratory, AAFS L12 and AAFS L14.
5. *Children's Jamaican Songs and Games,* Folkways Records, FC 7250.
6. *Children's Songs and Games,* from the Southern Mountains, Sung by Jean Ritchie — Folkways Records, FC 7059.
7. *Edna Ritchie,* (Viper, Kentucky), Folk-Legacy Records, Inc., FSA-3, Sharon, Connecticut.
8. *Folk Music from Wisconsin,* Library of Congress, Recording Laboratory, AAFS L55.
9. *Play and Dance Songs and Tunes,* Library of Congress, Recording Laboratory, AAFS L9.
10. *Ring Games, Line Games and Play Party Songs of Alabama,* Folkways Records, FC 7004.
11. *The Negro People in America,* Heirloom Records, 1964.

Educational Resources from Boosey & Hawkes

Bolkavec, E. and Johnson, J.	One Hundred Fifty Rounds for Singing and Teaching
Erdei, P. and Komlos, K.	One Hundred Fifty American Folk Songs to Sing, Read, and Play
Feierabend, J.	Music for Little People (book and tape) Music for Very Little People (book and tape)
Locke, E.	Sail Away - 155 American Folk Songs
Rao, D.	We Will Sing! - choral textbook - teacher's resource pack - accompaniment cassette and CD - performance cassette and CD - individual performance programs
Strong, A.	Who Was Kodály?
Tacka, P. and Houlahan, M.	Sound Thinking: Developing Musical Literacy (in two volumes) - Sight-Singing and Ear Training Materials (in two volumes)
Tacka, P. and Taylor-Howell, S.	Sourwood Mountain
Taylor-Howell, S.	The Owl Sings
Welles, J.	Managing Young Choirs Vol. 1: The Board of Directors; How to Provide the Chrous' Business Needs Vol. 2: Promoting and Fund Raising: How to Market and Finance the Chorus (this series will be continued)

Kodály Resources from Boosey & Hawkes

Edited and Translated by Dr. Percy Young	Bicinia Hungarica I - 60 Progressive Two Part Songs 333 Elementary Exercises in Sight Singing Epigrams Let Us Sing Correctly 333 Reading Exercises Tricinia Hungarica 15 Two Part Exercises 22 Two Part Exercises 33 Two Part Exercises 44 Two Part Exercises 77 Two Part Exercises
Revised English Editions by Geoffry Russell-Smith	Bicinia Hungarica I - 60 Progressive Two Part Songs Bicinia Hungarica II - 40 Progressive Two Part Songs Bicinia Hungarica III - 20 Progressive Two Part Songs Bicinia Hungarica IV - 60 Progressive Two Part Songs Epigrams 50 Nursery Songs Pentatonic Music I - 100 Hungarian Folk Songs Pentatonic Music II - 100 Little Marches Pentatonic Music III - 100 Cheremissian Melodies Pentatonic Music IV - 140 Chuvash Melodies 55 Two Part Exercises 66 Two Part Exercises
Bacon, D.	Let's Sing Together - Songs for 3, 4, and 5 year olds
Bertalotti, A.	Fifty Six Solfeggi
Molnar and Agocsy	Classical Canons - 230 Solfeggios
Szonyi, E.	Bicinia Americana I Musical Reading and Writing - pupil's books - teacher's manuals
Szonyi, E. and Kodály, Z.	Principles in Practice - an approach to music education through the Kodály method